FOUR CENTURIES
of AMERICAN
EDUCATION

DAVID BARTON

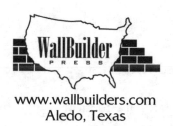

www.wallbuilders.com
Aledo, Texas

Additional materials available from:
WallBuilders, Inc., Post Office Box 397, Aledo, Texas 76008-0397
(817) 441-6044, www.wallbuilders.com

Cover illustration:
Gary Overacre
3802 Vineyard Trace
Marietta, GA 30062
(404) 973-8878

Cover design:
Dennis Gore
Hoyt Communications
5840 West I-20, Suite 200
Fort Worth, Texas 76017
(817) 563-0016

Library of Congress Cataloging-in-Publication Data

Barton, David
Four Centuries of American Education. Aledo, TX:
WallBuilder Press 2004
64 p; 21 cm.
ISBN 1-932225-32-3
Endnotes included.
LA205
1. Education   2. United States History   I. Title.

Printed in the United States of America

Four Centuries of American Education
by David Barton

America is now entering its fifth century of educating students. For every generation throughout the 17th, 18th, 19th, and 20th centuries, providing and obtaining a good education has been a major emphasis; it was that way when the first colonists arrived here four centuries ago, and that goal remains unchanged today in the 21st century.

But by what standard should a good education be measured? While some would measure it only by technological advances, it should also be measured by the content a student has learned – and by how well that student has been taught to think and to reason. Unfortunately, although the technological advances over the past fifty years have been significant, there is abundant evidence that the cognitive advances have lagged far behind.

EARLY ACADEMIC STANDARDS

Consider, for example, some of the fourth grade questions from an 1862 geography test in Chicago public schools:

How many degrees of longitude are there?

How many degrees wide are the temperate zones?

What is a watershed?

Name the principle animals of the frigid zones. [1]

FOURTH GRADE QUESTIONS.

GEOGRAPHY.

Thirty-five Minutes allowed for this Exercise.

[No books, nor helps of any kind, allowed on the desks, and none to be used during the Examination. All communication to be avoided. Pupils to receive no information from teachers, or others, respecting any of the questions. Every pupil to write at the top of each paper, his or her name, age in years and months, and name of the school; also *the grade of the questions used*, which will be found at the head of the questions. Each answer should be numbered to correspond with the number of the question. Pupils should be careful to express their answers in as good language as they can employ. They should also attend carefully to the spelling and writing, and to the use of capitals and marks of punctuation. All these points will be taken into account in summing up the results. Pupils of the third and fourth grades may either write or print their answers, as they prefer. At the close of the time specified every paper will be taken up, whether completed or not.]

1. How many degrees of longitude are there?
2. How many degrees wide are the temperate zones?
3. What is a water-shed?
4. Name the principal animals of the frigid zones.
5. Name the different races into which mankind is divided.
6. What is a monarchy?
7. What portion of the people on the globe are Pagans? What portion Christians?

CHICAGO, March 27, 1862.

(While these questions were reflective of basic fourth grade knowledge in 1862, today this material is studied only in much higher grades – if at all.)

Consider also the basic math content of previous generations. *Ray's Arithmetic* was one of the most popular elementary math texts in early American schools; notice some of its questions:

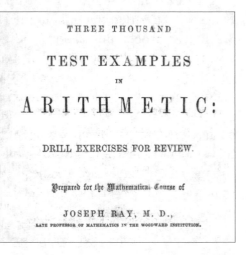

THREE THOUSAND

TEST EXAMPLES

IN

ARITHMETIC:

DRILL EXERCISES FOR REVIEW.

Prepared for the Mathematical Course of

JOSEPH RAY, M. D.,

LATE PROFESSOR OF MATHEMATICS IN THE WOODWARD INSTITUTION.

> I insured 2/3 of a shop worth $3600, and 4/5 of a house worth $6000, paying $126: what was the rate of insurance?

> How much money must be given with nine $100 shares at 15% discount, in exchange for eight $100 bonds at 2% discount? [2]

These were <u>elementary</u> math problems during the 1860s!

Consider also the math problems from an 1877 mental math text (that is, a text in which students solved the problems mentally – no pencil or paper allowed):

> A boat worth $864 – of which 1/8 belonged to A, 1/4 to B, and the rest to C – was lost; what loss did each sustain, it having been insured for $500?

> On a farm, there are 60 animals – horses, cows, and sheep; for each horse there are 3 cows, and for each cow there are 2 sheep: how many animals of each kind? [3]

> If 7 men can do a piece of work in 4 days, in what time can it be done if 3 of the men leave when the work is half completed? [4]

These were mental math problems for elementary students in 1877!

Consider the questions in an 1882 history text:

> What is a "writ of habeas corpus?"
> What is a bill of attainder?
> What is an ex-post-facto law?
> Enumerate the powers denied to the several States.
> What are bills of credit? [5]

1001

QUESTIONS AND ANSWERS

ON

UNITED STATES HISTORY;

INCLUDING THE

CONSTITUTION AND AMENDMENTS.

———

BY

B. A. HATHAWAY.

THE BURROWS BROTHERS COMPANY,
CLEVELAND, OHIO.

How many of today's elementary students – or, for that matter, how many adults in this so-called modern and advanced age – could answer these questions from a century ago?

One final example of the educational rigor of previous generations is illustrated by the *Federalist Papers*. [6] Written in 1787-1788 by three prominent Founding Fathers (James Madison, Alexander Hamilton, and John Jay) to explain why a federal Constitution was needed, even today this work is still considered the single most authoritative source on the intent of the Constitution.

A law professor in Alabama [7] currently requires his law students to read the *Federalist Papers*. And why not? Before those students can be-

FEDERALIST PAPERS AUTHORS: JAMES MADISON (L), JOHN JAY (C), ALEXANDER HAMILTON (R)

come attorneys, they will swear an oath to uphold the Constitution; so why not learn about
the intent of the document they will swear
to uphold? Those law students – enrolled in
<u>graduate</u> level studies – regularly complain to
him about the difficulty of reading that work.
He nods sympathetically and responds, "I
understand. This book was not written for
someone at your educational level; this book
was written for the common, average, upstate
New York farmer of 1787. Perhaps some day
you will attain the educational level of those
early New York farmers!"

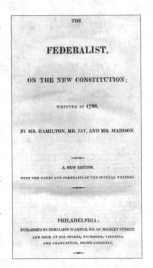

THE

FEDERALIST,

ON THE NEW CONSTITUTION;

WRITTEN IN 1788,

BY MR. HAMILTON, MR. JAY, AND MR. MADISON.

A NEW EDITION,

WITH THE NAMES AND PORTRAITS OF THE SEVERAL WRITERS.

PHILADELPHIA:
PUBLISHED BY BENJAMIN WARNER, NO. 147, MARKET STREET,
AND SOLD AT HIS STORES, RICHMOND, VIRGINIA,
AND CHARLESTON, SOUTH CAROLINA.

Early American Education

Indisputably, our early educational system was remarkable; and since
an ancient axiom accurately notes, "The philosophy of the schoolroom
in one generation will be the philosophy of government in the next,"
it is appropriate to examine closely the educational philosophy that
produced the longest on-going constitutional republic in the history
of the world. What was the educational philosophy of the schools
from which our early leaders graduated?

Harvard was one school that trained a number of those leaders,
including signers of the Declaration such as John Adams, John
Hancock, Samuel Adams, William Ellery, William Hooper, Robert
Treat Paine, William Williams, and Elbridge Gerry; signers of the
Constitution such as William Samuel Johnson and Rufus King; and
other prominent leaders, including Fisher Ames (a framer of the
Bill of Rights), William Cushing (an original justice on the U. S.
Supreme Court), and Timothy Pickering (an American general dur-
ing the Revolution and the Secretary of War for Presidents George
Washington and John Adams). [8]

Significantly, Harvard was established as a school to train ministers
of the Gospel; and its educational philosophy was clearly set forth in

Harvard University

Early Harvard Graduates

JOHN HANCOCK

WILLIAM HOOPER

ROBERT TREAT PAINE

WILLIAM ELLERY

SAMUEL ADAMS

JOHN ADAMS

FISHER AMES

TIMOTHY PICKERING

its two mottoes: "For Christ and the Church" and "For the Glory of Christ." [9] Consistent with those two mottoes, Harvard admonished:

> Let every student be plainly instructed and . . . consider well, the main end of his life and studies is to know God and Jesus, which is eternal life (JOHN 17:3), and therefore to lay Christ in the bottom as the only foundation of all sound knowledge and learning. [10]

HARVARD LOGO

To help students place Christ as the "foundation of . . . knowledge and learning," Harvard instituted specific educational practices, including:

> Everyone shall so exercise himself in reading the Scriptures twice a day that he shall be ready to give such an account of his proficiency therein. [11]

At Harvard – a school that trained a significant number of those who established our philosophy of government – academic endeavors were built upon the foundation of Biblical principles.

Yale was another popular school of that day and, like Harvard, it began as a school to train ministers of the Gospel. Yale produced signers of the Declaration such as Lyman Hall, Philip Livingston, Lewis Morris, and Oliver Wolcott; signers of the Constitution such as Abraham Baldwin, Jared Ingersoll, and William Livingston; and other prominent leaders, including Noah Webster (a famous educator and the author of the dictionary that still bears his name), Zephaniah Swift (author of the first American legal text), and James Kent (a leading judge, called the "Father of American Jurisprudence"). [12]

Yale admonished its students:

> Above all, have an eye to the great end of all your studies, which is to obtain the clearest conceptions of Divine things and to lead you to a saving knowledge of God in his Son Jesus Christ. [13]

Yale University

Early Yale Graduates

LEWIS MORRIS

WILLIAM LIVINGSTON

JARED INGERSOLL

LYMAN HALL

OLIVER WOLCOTT

NOAH WEBSTER

ABRAHAM BALDWIN

PHILIP LIVINGSTON

In pursuit of this goal, Yale stipulated:

> All the scholars are required to live a religious and blameless life according to the rules of God's Word, diligently reading the holy Scriptures . . . and constantly attending all the duties of religion. [14]

Yale, like Harvard, provided an education based on knowing Christ and studying Biblical principles.

Perhaps the school that produced more early national leaders than any other was Princeton. Also started as a school to train ministers of the Gospel, it produced signers of the Declaration such as Richard Stockton and Benjamin Rush; signers of the Constitution such as Gunning Bedford, Jr., Jonathan Dayton, James Madison, and William Paterson; and other prominent early leaders, including Oliver Ellsworth (a Chief Justice of the U. S. Supreme Court), Henry Lee (a general in the American Revolution known as "Light Horse Harry" Lee), and William Bradford (the U. S. Attorney General under President George Washington). [15]

Many Princeton graduates were personally trained by the university president, John Witherspoon, who was himself a signer of the Declaration. [†] What did Witherspoon require of students at Princeton?

> Every student shall attend worship in the college hall morning and evening. . . . [and] shall attend public worship on the Sabbath. . . . [T]here shall be assigned to each class certain exercises for their religious instruction. . . . and no student belonging to any class shall neglect them. [17]

REV. JOHN WITHERSPOON

---

† John Witherspoon may have trained more influential early American leaders than any other individual, for of the students that he personally instructed, one became a U. S. President, one a Vice-President, three became Supreme Court Justices, 13 were governors, and at least 20 became senators and 30 more became congressmen – not to mention several presidential cabinet members as well. [16] Dr. Witherspoon may rightly be called the educational father of many Founding Fathers.

Princeton University

Early Princeton Graduates

DR. BENJAMIN RUSH

RICHARD STOCKTON

WILLIAM BRADFORD

JONATHAN DAYTON

JAMES MADISON

WILLIAM PATERSON

HENRY LEE

GUNNING BEDFORD, JR.

Witherspoon personally instructed students:

> [H]e is the best friend to American liberty who is most sincere and active in promoting true and undefiled religion and who sets himself with the greatest firmness to bear down profanity and immorality of every kind. Whoever is an avowed enemy of God, I scruple [hesitate] not to call him an enemy to his country. [18]

Dr. Witherspoon understood that which was universally accepted by all knowledgeable individuals: government was merely a reflection of its citizens; if Americans became profane and immoral, their government would also become profane and immoral; and history has demonstrated conclusively that such governments do not survive. Consequently, it was simple logic that any true friend of America would promote religion and morality. †

Prominent American educators routinely equipped students with a Biblical foundation as part of academic instruction. In fact, so committed were they to inculcating these principles in all citizens

---

† Famous Princeton alumnus Elias Boudinot (a President of Congress and a framer of the Bill of Rights in the first Congress) was one of many national leaders who endorsed this same truth when he declared: "If the moral character of a people once degenerates, their political character must soon follow." [19]

Signer of the Declaration Samuel Adams agreed: "Neither the wisest constitution nor the wisest laws will secure the liberty and happiness of a people whose manners are universally corrupt." [20]

Bill of Rights framer Fisher Ames echoed: "Our liberty depends on . . . morals and religion, whose authority reigns in the heart – and on the influence all these produce on public opinion before that opinion governs rulers." [21]

Signer of the Declaration Charles Carroll similarly pronounced: "Without morals, a republic cannot subsist any length of time; they therefore who are decrying the Christian religion, whose morality is so sublime and pure . . . are undermining the solid foundation of morals, the best security for the duration of free governments." [22]

And President George Washington asserted: "Of all the dispositions and habits which lead to political prosperity, religion and morality are indispensable supports. In vain would that man claim the tribute of patriotism who should labor to subvert these great pillars of human happiness." [23]

Numerous other leaders and statesmen were equally adamant in proclaiming the principle that it was religion and morality, not constitutions and laws, that were the true foundation of successful American government.

that they even pioneered new educational venues, founding some of the first schools for women and for black Americans – something unprecedented at that time in world history.

For example, John Witherspoon personally trained a number of black American students at Princeton, [24] including John Chavis, [25] who went on to become a famous preacher and educator in North Carolina. And Francis Hopkinson and Benjamin Franklin (signers of the

Declaration) were also instrumental in the early development of African American education, [26] helping found a series of schools that trained African American students both in academics and in the principles of Christi-

BENJAMIN FRANKLIN (L) AND FRANCIS HOPKINSON (R)
PIONEERED AFRICAN AMERICAN EDUCATION

anity. [27] Furthermore,

Benjamin Rush (also a signer of the Declaration) not only promoted African American education [28] but also helped open education for women and was closely involved with the first American school to educate women. [29] These Founding Fathers (and many others) pioneered for _all_ children – regardless of race or gender – an education based on the inculcation of Biblical principles.

EARLY EDUCATIONAL LAWS

This educational philosophy promoting religious principles had not been introduced by the Founding Fathers (even though they strongly promoted it); that philosophy of education had been introduced a century-and-a-half earlier through America's educational laws.

America's first public education law had resulted from the experiences of the early settlers who arrived in America. They were

not only acutely aware of
the broader civil atroci-
ties in Europe that had
preceded them (such as
the Inquisition and the
tortures during the Cru-
sades – atrocities too often
perpetrated under the banner of Christianity) but

many had also personally experienced harsh persecution simply for
practicing their faith. [†] America's early immigrants were convinced
that the widespread illiteracy and lack of Biblical knowledge that
characterized Europe had been at the root of these atrocities.

[†] Official state - or church - sanctioned persecution against those Christians not of the
established church occurred across the centuries under both Catholic and Protestant regimes.
The earliest persecution waged against non-conforming Christians was by Catholics through
Papal inquisitions well before the emergence of Protestantism. Several Catholic Popes both
practiced and endorsed tyrannical persecutions, officially condoning the killings of dissenters
and burnings at the stake. Such actions even predated Pope Lucius III's 1184 AD establishment of an official Catholic office of the Inquisition. (It was not until 1962 that Pope John
XXIII closed that office.) Pope Gregory IX and several subsequent Popes had declared the
Bible off-limits to anyone but priests, and Popes such as Pius V and Sixtus V had actually
served as chief inquisitors before their ascension to the papacy.

The Protestant Reformation of the 15th century was a movement that originated when
some Catholic priests advocated adherence to the Scriptures rather than the Pope as the
primary authority for Christian life and living. These reformers placed an emphasis on
every individual Christian's reading, studying, and knowing the Bible personally, and on
each believer's praying directly to and having direct access to God (a doctrine called "the
priesthood of the believer"). The reaction to the Reformation by many church and state
leaders was often bloody, reflecting their intent to eradicate religious opposition through
the most oppressive measures.

For example, Henry VIII declared himself the head of the church in England and began
eradicating those of differing beliefs: Dutch Anabaptists were burned at the stake; other
religious leaders were charged with treason and executed; and Henry seized the property of
churches not affiliated with the Church of England. Subsequent kings, including King James,
conducted similar purges, mutilating, hanging, or disemboweling religious non-conformists
up until (and after) the time that the non-conformist Pilgrims and Puritans left for America
in search of religious freedom.

English Catholic leaders such as Queen Mary also conducted purges, including the
execution of John Rogers, who had assisted in the publication of Tyndale's English transla-

The civil and religious leaders in Europe had wrongly taught the masses that the Bible authorized such atrocities that it further authorized individual leaders of church and state to wield great and often tyrannical power over the people. Because the people were illiterate and therefore could not read the Scriptures to judge the accuracy of what their leaders told them, they blindly believed and followed, thus indirectly abetting the commission of those atrocities.

Learning from these tragedies, the American settlers were convinced that if the common people could read and learn the Word of God for themselves, and study the limits on governing authorities set forth in the Bible, citizens would

tions of the Scriptures. Following the Reformation, Protestants became a target for Catholic officials, who focused their attention on the eradication or suppression of Protestantism. For example, Spain attacked England with the Spanish Armada to effect a forcible conversion of Protestants to Catholicism; and in Germany, the Catholic attacks on Protestants led to the Thirty-Years War. Such efforts almost completely eradicated Protestantism in several nations, including Italy, Spain, and France.

It was from this history of persecution that so many religious settlers came to America; America became a land to receive the persecuted from across the world. For example, the Pilgrims came to America in 1620 to escape the hounding persecution of England's King James, and a decade later the Puritans (some 20,000) also came to America after Puritan laymen in England received life sentences (as well as having their noses slit, ears cut off, and a brand placed on their foreheads). Similarly, in 1632, Catholics persecuted in England fled to America; in 1654 Jews persecuted by Catholics and facing the Inquisition in Portugal fled to America; in 1680, Quakers fled to America after some 10,000 had been imprisoned or tortured in England for their faith; in 1683, persecuted German Anabaptists (Mennonites, Moravians, Dunkers, etc.) fled to America; in 1685, Huguenots fled France (eventually some 400,000) to avoid death and persecution from Catholic leaders; in 1731, 20,000 Lutherans fled to America after being expelled from Austria; and the story of persecution has been often repeated across the pages of history. America indeed was (and still is) a place of asylum chosen by the Almighty for the benefit of those in the rest of the world who were persecuted for their faith in God.

resist government misbehavior and thus preclude similar occurrences in America. [†] Therefore, in 1642 they passed America's first public education law: "The Old Deluder Satan Act." That law declared:

> It being one chief project of that old deluder, Satan, to keep men from the knowledge of the Scriptures, as in former time . . . [41]

SCHOOLES.

It being one cheife project of that old deluder, Sathan, to keepe men from the knowledge of the scriptures, as in former times, keeping them in an unknowne tongue, so in these latter times, by

AMERICA'S FIRST PUBLIC EDUCATION LAW, 1642

---

† While knowing and applying Biblical guidelines certainly did not prevent all atrocities, it indisputably reduced them. Despite the fact that critics point to a few genuine atrocities perpetrated, or even allegedly perpetrated, in the name of Christianity (e.g., the witch trials in Salem, Massachusetts, and across the rest of the world; the expulsion and torture of Moors; the Inquisition; and even the World War II Holocaust (which some Jews attribute to Christians since Hitler was at one time a member of a Christian church), it is nevertheless irrefutable that those without Christian influence have committed countless more atrocities.

(Despite the fact that some Holocaust survivors believe Hitler to have been a Christian, recent documentation made available from the OSS (the noted intelligence agency of World War II), proves that Hitler was anti-Christian and that the Nazis engaged in a systematic campaign to eradicate European Christianity. [30] Furthermore, Hitler killed more than twice as many Gentiles as Jews, [31] and both he and the Nazi party were linked to anti-Biblical occultism. [32])

If one tabulates the loss of lives occasioned by "Christian" conduct (excluding Hitler, since it is proved that he was anti-Christian), the total which may be laid at the doorstep of Christianity over the past two thousand years is well _under_ 5 million; however, the number of lives lost at the hands of non- and anti-Christian leaders in just the 20th century alone is _over_ one-hundred million. Consider the 62 million killed during the 20th century by Soviet Communists; the 35 million by Communist Chinese; the 1.7 million by the Vietnamese Communists; the 1 million in the Polish Ethnic Cleansing; the 1 million in Yugoslavia; the 1.7 million in North Korea, [33] etc. – all non- or anti-Christian regimes.

Furthermore, consider the deaths perpetrated by individual anti-Christian leaders. For example, Joseph Stalin was responsible for the murder of 42.7 million; Mao Tse-tung, 37.8 million; Hitler, 20.9 million; Vladimir Lenin, 4 million; Tojo Hideki, 4 million; Pol Pot of the Khmer Rouge, 1 million; Yahya Khan, 1.5 million; [34] and numerous other anti-Christian leaders could be listed. Therefore, while the lives lost at the hands of Christians in the past two thousand years regrettably may number in the millions, the number lost at the hands of anti-Christians is more than 20 times greater, and in only five percent of the time (i.e., in just the past one hundred years).

Furthermore, the lives lost under the guise of "Christianity" should be categorized in greater detail. For example, historian Daniel Dorchester pointed out that although inhumanities have occurred in the name of Christianity, very few have occurred under the banner of American Christianity:

> These "dreadful and disgusting inhumanities" were perpetrated by whom? Refined and cultivated Europeans. . . . Such are the facts of modern history which should moderate our denunciations and charges of severity, brutality and narrow-mindedness against the colonial forefathers, who, it clearly appears, were much in advance of their times. [35]

Perhaps the single most famous American atrocity perpetrated in the name of Christianity was the Massachusetts witch trials. In that episode spanning 4 months, some 21 deaths occurred. (Incidentally, that number is surpassed by the recent shootings at public schools in Columbine, Colorado, and West Paducah, Kentucky, and by the church shooting in Wedgewood, Texas, in which anti-religious individuals killed more than were put to death in the notorious 1692 episode. [36] And while some 21 individuals were victims of the American witch trials, about half-a-million were put to death in the European witch trials. [37] Therefore, America – despite its faults – was still far better than the "civilized" Old World at the same time. Nevertheless, textbooks often dwell upon that single American atrocity while ignoring anti-Christian atrocities much larger in scope.) The Massachusetts witch trials were brought to a close when Christian leaders such as Rev. Increase Mather and Thomas Brattle invoked Christian teachings, thus convincing Governor Phipps to end the trials. [38]

Ironically, the charge of the harmfulness of Christianity to a society is not new; when that claim was raised two hundred years ago, signer of the Declaration John Witherspoon responded forcefully:

> Let us try it by its fruits. Let us compare the temper and character of real Christians with those of infidels and see which of them best merits the approbation of an honest and impartial judge. Let us take in every circumstance that will contribute to make the comparison just and fair and see what will be the result. . . . In which of the two is to be found the greatest integrity and uprightness in their conduct between man and man? the most unfeigned good-will? and the most active beneficence to others? Is it the unbeliever or the Christian who clothes the naked and deals his bread to the hungry? Ask the many and noble ancient structures raised for the relief of the diseased and the poor to whom they owe their establishment and supports. [39]

The results, or what Witherspoon called the "fruits," do indeed speak for themselves. While Christianity certainly does not make men perfect, yet – as is demonstrable both historically and statistically – it does tend to restrain their inherent destructive behavior. As Ben Franklin once reminded religious critic Thomas Paine:

> If men are so wicked with religion, what would they be if without it? [40]

Clearly, the plan of the early colonists to prevent civil atrocities by inculcating a knowledge of the Scriptures in all citizens was not only laudable in theory but also sound in practice.

Having set forth the purpose of the law and the evil it was designed to prevent, the law then required that public schools be started in each community so that American students would receive a sound academic education based on God's Word. This Bible-centered emphasis in education was common in subsequent education laws as well – a fact confirmed by the records of foreign visitors to America.

Foreign observers often would travel to America to investigate what had caused her remarkable progress and rapid rise. As they traveled throughout the colonies, they would document various customs and practices and then return to their native countries to publish the results of their investigations.

One such foreign visitor was Briton Edward Kendall. [42] As he traveled from region to region, he documented the diverse aspects of American life – from courts of justice to Indian missions, from prison systems to theaters and public entertainments. While in Connecticut, Kendall examined American education and found the State's illiteracy law of interest – particularly the opening declaration of that law:

> This [legislature] observing that not withstanding our former orders made for the education of children . . . there are many persons unable to read the English tongue, and thereby incapable of reading the Holy Word of God or the good laws of this [State]. . . . [43]

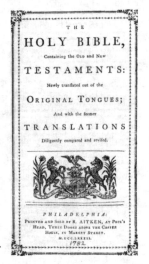

The Connecticut legislature had been concerned about illiteracy because if a child could not read, then he would not know the Word of God or the laws of the State. Therefore, if the legislature enacted a law that contradicted the Word of God, and if citizens were illiterate and uneducated about the proper role of civil government as set forth in the Scriptures, they might not prevent the passage of that inappropriate law.

Frenchman Alexis de Tocqueville also reported the same fact about the religious aspect of American public education. His famous work, originally called *The Republic of the United States of America and Its Political Institutions, Reviewed and Examined,* [44] is today known as *Democracy in America.* [45] His observations in that work fully confirm the religious nature of American public education. [46]

ALEXIS DE TOCQUEVILLE AND HIS FAMOUS BOOK ABOUT AMERICA

Another famous early law was "The Northwest Ordinance" – the first federal law to address education. Significantly, that law was passed at the same time and by the identical Founding Fathers who drafted the First Amendment – the very Amendment that courts now interpret as prohibiting the presence of religious activities in public education. Even today, that law is still considered one of the four organic – or fundamental – American laws on which all others are to be based. [47]

Article III of that federal law (signed by President George Washington) directly linked religion and public education together, declaring:

> Religion, morality, and knowledge, being necessary to good government and the happiness of mankind, schools and the means of education shall forever be encouraged. [48]

The Founders believed – and in this first federal education law acknowledged – that schools and education systems were a proper means to encourage the "religion, morality, and knowledge" that was so "necessary to good government and the happiness of mankind." The framers of our government did not believe that encouraging religion in

AMERICAN EDUCATION INCULCATED
RELIGION, MORALITY, AND KNOWLEDGE

schools was unconstitutional; rather, they believed just the opposite; only in recent decades have courts ruled otherwise.

The effect of that first federal law was quite evident in early State constitutions, for compliance with that law was a pre-requisite for the admission of a territory as a State into the Union. [49] Therefore, when Ohio adopted its first State constitution in 1802, that document declared:

> Religion, morality, and knowledge, being essentially necessary to the good government, and the happiness of mankind, schools and the means of instruction shall forever be encouraged by legislative provision. [50]

The same provision was present in the constitutions of State after State, including Mississippi, [51] Kansas, [52] Nebraska, [53] and many others. In fact, that provision is still found in numerous State constitutions today. [54]

An 1893 book documenting American educational history further confirms the inclusion of "religion, morality, and knowledge" throughout our educational system. That book was prepared as part of the international celebration of the 400th anniversary of Columbus Day in 1892, an event celebrated that year with a huge international festival in Chicago. Many of the trades and professions represented at that

COLUMBUS LANDING IN
THE WESTERN WORLD IN 1492

festival prepared records of their progress over the previous four centuries, and it was the Kansas teachers' association that prepared a review of the history of education in America. [55]

CHURCHES WERE THE CENTER OF EDUCATION IN AMERICA

That historical overview first observed that American education was "[n]urtured in the lap of the church," [56] and then noted that as the nation grew and the number of inhabitants in America increased, "the church reluctantly relinquished her claim upon the elementary schools." [57] Yet, despite the fact that the jurisdictional authority over education had been partially shifted and was being shared with the State, the philosophy of education remained unchanged. In fact, the State superintendent of public instruction even warned:

THE SUPERINTENDENT OF PUBLIC INSTRUCTION

[I]f the study of the Bible is to be excluded from all State schools – if the inculcation of the principles of Christianity is to have no place in the daily program – if the worship of God is to form no part of the general exercises of these public elementary schools – then the good of the State would be better served by restoring all schools to church control. [58]

Government education leaders believed that if public education ever became so secular that it did not inculcate religion, morality, and knowledge – if public schools did not teach the Bible, inculcate the principles of Christianity, and incorporate the daily worship of God – then the nation would be better off if the State gave all its schools back to the church.

An indication of how long religious lessons remained a part of public education in America is seen in two textbooks used in Dallas Public Schools: a *Bible Study Course of the Old Testament* and a *Bible Study Course of the New Testament* [†] (both were credit courses for

---

† Both of these Bible study courses have been reprinted by WallBuilders and are available for schools, church, or home through the online store at www.wallbuilders.com or by calling 1-800-873-2845.

graduation used until 1974, and were also used in other major school districts across the nation, including Indianapolis, St. Louis, Little Rock, etc.). "Lesson 1" in the New Testament course begins by having students read John 1 and then answer questions such as:

> "Where was Christ before he was born on earth?"
>
> "What titles does John apply to Christ in this chapter?"
>
> "For what purpose was John sent by God?"
>
> "Name five things the angel told Mary concerning her child Jesus?"
>
> "What does the word Jesus mean?" [59]

There are hundreds of similar questions throughout the course. At the end of each lesson is memory work. For example, in Lesson 1:

> Memorize the pre-existence of Christ: "In the beginning was the Word, and the Word was with God and the Word was God. All things were made by Him and without Him was not anything made that was made." [JOHN 1:1,3] [60]

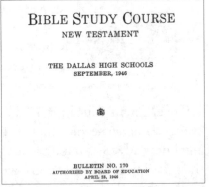

Such public school textbooks were reflective of the requirements of the original 1789 federal law that schools address "religion, morality, and knowledge." Religious principles were universally considered to be an inseparable part of a sound public education, whether at the elementary or the university level.

In fact, at the university level in 1860, 262 out of 288 college presidents were ministers of the Gospel – as were more than a third of all university faculty members. [61] And in 1890, James Angell,

President of the University of Vermont and the University of Michigan, reported that over 90 percent of the State universities conducted chapel services; at half, chapel attendance was compulsory; and a quarter required regular church attendance *in addition* to chapel attendance. [62] Well into the 20th century, this remained the practice of State universities – a practice that was simply the continuation of the philosophy of education that had caused America to become the most successful and prosperous nation in the history of the world.

EARLY EDUCATIONAL PIONEERS

Many of America's early educational leaders were patriots who had been directly involved in the American Revolution. They understood that if America was to endure beyond the Revolution, then the principles on which she had been birthed, nurtured, and developed must be successfully transmitted to future generations; [63] and it was for this reason that so many of them became directly involved in writing educational plans, authoring textbooks, or starting universities. [64] In fact, there were more universities established in America in the ten years following the Revolution than in the 150 years before. [65]

DR. BENJAMIN RUSH

One such early educational leader was Dr. Benjamin Rush, a signer of the Declaration of Independence who also served in three presidential administrations. [66] Dr. Rush had helped found five colleges [67] (three of which still exist today); he was also a university professor, authored numerous textbooks, and was among the first Founding Fathers to propose nationwide public schools, [68] for which he may be titled "The Father of Public Schools under the Constitution."

Like most of the other Founding Fathers, Dr. Rush was a prolific writer; and one of his educational policy papers was titled, "A Defense of the Use of the Bible in Schools" (1791). [†] At the beginning of that work, Dr. Rush first declared:

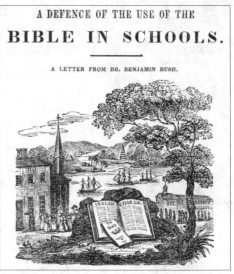

A DEFENCE OF THE USE OF THE

BIBLE IN SCHOOLS.

A LETTER FROM DR. BENJAMIN RUSH.

> Before I state my arguments in favor of teaching children to read by means of the Bible, I shall assume the five following propositions: I. – That Christianity is the only true and perfect religion, and that in proportion as mankind adopts its principles and obeys its precepts, they will be wise and happy; II. – That a better knowledge of this religion is to be acquired by reading the Bible than in any other way; III. – That the Bible contains more knowledge necessary to man in his present state than any other book in the world; IV. – That knowledge is most durable and religious instruction most useful when imparted in early life; and V. – That the Bible, when not read in schools, is seldom read in any subsequent period of life. [69]

Dr. Rush next set forth nearly a dozen reasons why the Bible should always remain the cardinal textbook of American education; he then closed his piece with a succinct warning on what would happen in America if the Bible were removed from schools:

---

† Dr. Rush's work has been reprinted by WallBuilders and is available as a small pamphlet through the online store at www.wallbuilders.com or by calling 1-800-873-2845.

In contemplating the political institutions of the United States, I lament that [if we remove the Bible from schools] we waste so much time and money in punishing crimes and take so little pains to prevent them. . . . For this Divine Book, above all others, favors that equality among mankind, that respect for just laws, and those sober and frugal virtues which constitute the soul of [our government]. [70]

Dr. Rush correctly saw the Bible as the only sure means to prevent crime, for it dealt with the heart – the source of all crime; he therefore accurately forewarned that if America ceased to teach the Bible in schools, then not only would crime increase but great quantities of time and money would be expended in fighting crime.

Another famous Founder with clear views on education was Gouverneur Morris – a signer of the Constitution and the most active member of the Constitutional Convention. [71] In fact, Morris was chosen by his peers at the Convention to take their rough ideas and create the final language that appeared in the Constitution and he is therefore titled, "The Penman of the Constitution." [72] Notice his recommendation on education:

> Religion is the only solid basis of good morals; therefore, education should teach the precepts of religion and the duties of man towards God. [73]

GOUVERNEUR MORRIS
"PENMAN OF THE CONSTITUTION"

The penman of our Constitution believed that it was appropriate for schools to teach religion.

Another important early leader with strong views on education was Fisher Ames. Ames helped frame the Bill of Rights and proposed the final wording for the First Amendment as passed by the House of Representatives in 1789. [74] His early published writings include an article entitled "School Books" in which he commented on a growing trend he had observed in American education:

> It has been the custom of late years to put a number of little books into the hands of children, containing fables and moral lessons. This is very well because it is right first to raise curiosity and then to guide it. [75]

SCHOOL BOOKS.

First published in the Palladium, January, 1801.

IT has been the custom, of late years, to put a number of little books into the hands of children, containing fables and moral lessons. This is very well, because it is right first to raise curiosity, and then to guide it. Many books for children are, however, injudiciously compiled: the language is too much raised above the ideas of that tender age; the moral is drawn from the fable, they know not why; and when they gain wisdom from experience, they will see the restrictions and exceptions which are necessary to the rules of

However, Ames pointed out a dangerous unintended consequence of placing more books into the hands of children. He explained that each time a new book was added to the classroom, time was spent on that new book; the growing amount of time spent on the many new books could eventually reduce the time students spent on the Bible. To this possibility, Ames strongly objected:

FISHER AMES

> Why then, if these books for children must be retained (as they will be), should not the Bible regain the place it once held as a school book? Its morals are pure; its examples, captivating and noble. The reverence for the Sacred Book that is thus early impressed lasts long, and probably, if not impressed in infancy, never takes firm hold of the mind. [76]

Fisher Ames – a primary author of the First Amendment (which the courts now wrongly interpret as a constitutional mandate for a secular society through their misapplication of "separation of church and state") – warned that the Bible must never be pushed to the back of the classroom, much less completely out of schools. A number of other early statesmen and educators agreed that the study of the Bible was an indispensable part of a good education.

For example, John Quincy Adams, a U. S. President and a university professor at Harvard, had declared:

> To a man of liberal education, . . . with regard to the history contained in the Bible . . . "it is not so much praiseworthy to be acquainted with as it is shameful to be ignorant of it." [77]

Founding Father Henry Laurens, a President of Congress, similarly declared:

> [T]he Bible. . . . [is] a necessary part of a polite education. [78]

And Dr. Benjamin Rush echoed:

> [T]he Bible . . . should be read in our schools in preference to all other books. [79]

Tragically, today the Bible has been pushed not just to the back of the classroom but completely out of it [80] – supposedly in the name and by the authority of the same early leaders who worked so hard to put and keep the Bible in the classroom.

Noah Webster was another famous American with a significant impact on education. He had been a soldier during the American Revolution, a legislator and a judge following the Revolution, and he directly impacted the final wording of the Constitution. [81] As an educator, he helped found Amherst College and authored scores of textbooks on a variety of different subjects, [82] including the famous dictionary that bears his name. His impact on education was so profound that he has been titled, "The Schoolmaster to America." [83]

NOAH WEBSTER AMHERST COLLEGE

The first textbook penned by Webster was his famous speller. [84]
Introduced in 1783, it became <u>the</u> spelling book for American schools
for the next 150 years. In later years, that
speller was popularly known as *Webster's
Blue Back Speller* because of the distinc-
tive blue color of its cover.

In Webster's early spellers, every page
– including the cover page and the fly
leaf – was filled with useful information.
And what did Webster print on those
pages that today are usually blank? On
the inside of his 1839 speller he used Bible
verses – specifically the lengthy passage
from Ecclesiastes 12, beginning with:

> Remember now thy Creator in the
> days of thy youth, while the evil days
> come not, nor the years draw nigh,
> when thou shall say, I have no plea-
> sure in them, &c. [85]

**BACK COVER OF
WEBSTER'S 1839 SPELLER**

Yet it was no surprise that Noah Webster placed the Scriptures in
his texts, for his philosophy of education was clear:

> The Christian religion is the most important and one of
> the first things in which all children under a free govern-
> ment ought to be instructed. . . . No truth is more evident
> to my mind than that the Christian religion must be the
> basis of any government intended to secure the rights and
> privileges of a free people. [86]

Webster's school texts therefore not only included rigorous academic
exercises but they also contained moral and religious lessons. [87] And
Webster did not hesitate to acknowledge the important role that
Christianity had played in the establishment of America as a successful
independent nation. For example, in his *History of the United States*

– a famous text long used in public schools – Webster taught students:

> The brief exposition of the Constitution of the United States will unfold to young persons the principles of republican government; and ... our citizens should early understand that the genuine source of correct republican principles is the Bible – particularly the New Testament or the Christian religion. [88]

Webster concluded by reminding students how important it was to America that citizens observe the precepts of the Bible:

> [T]he moral principles and precepts contained in the Scriptures ought to form the basis of all of our civil constitutions and laws.... All of the miseries and evils which men suffer from vice, crime, ambition, injustice, oppression, slavery and war, proceed from them despising or neglecting the precepts contained in the Bible. [89]

So strongly did Webster advocate sound education inculcating religion and morality that the epitaph given him in textbooks following his death was an accurate tribute to his educational philosophy: "Who taught millions to read, not one to sin." [90]

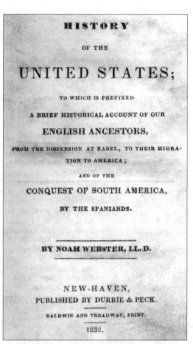

HISTORY

OF THE

UNITED STATES;

TO WHICH IS PREFIXED

A BRIEF HISTORICAL ACCOUNT OF OUR

ENGLISH ANCESTORS,

FROM THE DISPERSION AT BABEL, TO THEIR MIGRATION TO AMERICA;

AND OF THE

CONQUEST OF SOUTH AMERICA,

BY THE SPANIARDS.

BY NOAH WEBSTER, LL. D.

NEW-HAVEN,
PUBLISHED BY DURRIE & PECK.

BALDWIN AND TREADWAY, PRINT.

1832.

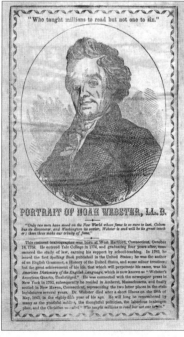

"Who taught millions to read but not one to sin."

PORTRAIT OF NOAH WEBSTER, LL. D.

Dr. Jedidiah Morse was another leading educator from the Founding Era. He was very active on the political scene throughout the Revolution, held government positions in the federal government after

the Revolution, and has been titled the "Father of American Geography" [91] for his specific contributions to American education (it was Morse who instituted the study of American geography in our schools). Jedidiah Morse – like Noah Webster – was a prolific writer of textbooks; he, too, had much to say about the importance of Christianity to our government. For example, Morse declared:

> To the kindly influence of Christianity we owe that degree of civil freedom and political and social happiness which mankind now enjoys. In proportion as the genuine effects of Christianity are diminished in any nation . . . in the same proportion will the people of that nation recede from the blessings of genuine freedom . . . I hold this to be a truth confirmed by experience; and it follows that all efforts made to destroy the foundations of our Holy Religion ultimately tend to the subversion also of our political freedom and happiness. Whenever the pillars of Christianity shall be overthrown, our present republican forms of government (and all the blessings which flow from them) must fall with them. [92]

DR. JEDIDIAH MORSE

Jedidiah Morse believed that if the influence of Christianity were lost in the nation, our political and social freedoms would also be lost.

George Washington was another strong supporter of sound education – a fact made clear throughout his presidency from his signing of the "Northwest Ordinance" in the first year of his presidency (1789) to his call for the establishment of national universities and academies in his last year (1796). [93] However, Washington's educational philosophy had been revealed long before his presidency.

GEORGE WASHINGTON

In 1779, Delaware Indian chiefs brought some of their youth to George Washington, asking that they be trained in America's schools. Washington received those youth, assuring the chiefs that "Congress . . . will look upon them as their own children" [94] – that is, that we would look after and train Indian youth with the same care and diligence that we exercised over our own children. Wash-

AMERICAN INDIAN EDUCATION

ington then commended the chiefs for their decision to bring their children to American schools, telling them:

> You do well to wish to learn our arts and our ways of life, and above all, the religion of Jesus Christ. These will make you a greater and happier people than you are; Congress will do everything they can to assist you in this wise intention. [95]

According to George Washington, what youth would learn in American schools "above all" was "the religion of Jesus Christ."

Samuel Adams, known as "The Father of the American Revolution," [96] also made significant contributions to American education. In a noted exchange of letters with his famous cousin, John Adams (who differed with Samuel on many political issues), Samuel set forth his educational policy:

> Let [ministers] and philosophers, statesmen and patriots, unite their endeavors to renovate the age by impressing the minds of men with the importance of educating their little boys and girls

– of inculcating in the minds of youth – . . . the love of their country; of instructing them in the art of self-government . . . [and] in short, of leading them in the study and practice of the exalted virtues of the Christian system. [97]

SAMUEL ADAMS   JOHN ADAMS

John Adams wrote back to Samuel and announced his concurrence with Samuel's plan, declaring to him that on this subject, "You and I agree." [98] However, not only did Samuel Adams recommend that students be instructed in Christian principles but he even helped teach those principles by reprinting for the classroom one of the most famous of all American schoolbooks, [99] *The New England Primer.* †

The New England Primer (the first textbook ever published in America [100]) was originally printed in Boston around 1690 and was reprinted frequently over the next two centuries – including the 1762 reprint by Samuel Adams. Well into the 20th century, *The New England Primer* remained a common text from which American students learned to read. [101] The *Primer* was the equivalent of a first-grade textbook. (Even though there were no grade levels in early American education at that time, the *Primer* was

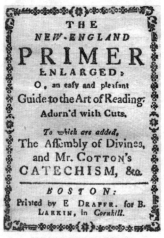

THE NEW ENGLAND PRIMER

the beginning reader – it was where students began their reading lessons; so today it would be called a first-grade textbook.)

Over its two centuries of use, the cover page of the *Primer* would change from edition to edition, but the *Primer* itself maintained

---

† *The New England Primer* has been reprinted by WallBuilders and is available through the online store at www.wallbuilders.com or by calling 1-800-873-2845.

THE

NEW-ENGLAND

PRIMER

IMPROVED

For the more eafy attaining the true
reading of Englifh.

TO WHICH IS ADDED

The Affembly of Divines, and
Mr. COTTON's *Catechifm.*

BOSTON:

Printed by EDWARD DRAPER, *at*
his Printing-Office, in *Newbury-*
Street, and *Sold* by JOHN BOYLE
in *Marlborough-Street.*   1777.

The Honorable JOHN HANCOCK, Efq;
Prefident of the *American* CONGRESS.

THE 1777 *NEW ENGLAND PRIMER*

THE
NEW-ENGLAND
PRIMER
ENLARGED:
O, an eafy and pleafant
Guide to the Art of Reading.
Adorn'd with Cuts.

To which are added,
The Affembly of Divines,
and Mr. COTTON's
CATECHISM, &c.

BOSTON:
Printed by E DRAPER. for B.
LARKIN, in *Cornhill.*

GENERAL WASHINGTON

THE 1795 *NEW ENGLAND PRIMER*

THE 1813 *NEW ENGLAND PRIMER*

THE 1820 *NEW ENGLAND PRIMER*

three core elements: the "Rhyming Alphabet," the "Alphabet of Lessons for Youth," and the "Shorter Catechism." Notice the content of the first core element – the "Rhyming Alphabet" – and recall that for two centuries this alphabet was a key part of public education in America:

A – In Adam's fall, we sinned all.

B – Heaven to find, the Bible mind.

C – Christ crucified, for sinners died, &c. [102]

THE RHYMING ALPHABET

The second key element of the *Primer* was the "Alphabet of Lessons for Youth." This section was the ABCs in a bold column running vertically down the page, with each letter of the alphabet accompanied by a Bible verse:

A – A wise son makes a glad father, but a foolish son is the heaviness of his mother [PROVERBS 10:1].

B – Better is a little with the fear of the Lord than great treasure and trouble therewith [PROVERBS 15:16].

C – Come unto Christ all ye that labor and are heavy laden, and He will give you rest [MATTHEW 11:28], &c. [103]

THE ALPHABET OF LESSONS

The third section common to the *Primer* was the "Shorter Catechism," and it contained questions such as:

"Which is the fifth commandment?"

"What is required in the fifth commandment?"

"What is forbidden in the fifth commandment?"

"What is the reason annexed to the fifth commandment?" [104]

(It is noteworthy that for centuries, the Ten Commandments were taught in America's public schools.)

Not only was *The New England Primer* reprinted by Samuel Adams for students in Massachusetts but it was also reprinted by Benjamin Franklin † for students in Pennsylvania. [105] The fact that Franklin was directly involved with personally distributing such an

DR. BENJAMIN FRANKLIN

overtly religious schoolbook might surprise many Americans today, for Franklin is considered to be one of the least religious of our Founding Fathers. (While Franklin certainly *is* one of the least religious Founders, ironically, he was definitely more religious than many so-called devoutly religious individuals today. ††) Franklin had long demonstrated his overt support for teaching Christian principles in public education.

For example, recall the fact already discussed (p. 13) that Franklin helped found schools in the 1760s in which African American students were taught not only academics but also the principles of Christianity. [106] And two decades before that, in 1740, Franklin had helped found the University of Pennsylvania for the explicitly declared purpose of instructing youth in the knowledge of the Christian religion. [107] Then in 1749, Franklin authored the famous piece entitled, *Proposals Relating to the Education of Youth in Pennsylvania* in which he discussed the content of the academic curriculum of the State's new university, noting that in its history classes:

> History will . . . afford frequent opportunities of showing the necessity of a public religion from its usefulness to the public [and] the advantage of a religious character among private persons . . . and the excellency of the Christian religion above all others, ancient or modern. [108]

---

† Franklin is one of the three faces depicted on the cover of this booklet, the farthest left of the three individuals.

†† For more information on the strongly religious activities of this "least religious" Founding Father, see the sections on Franklin in *The Role of Pastors and Christians in Civil Government* and *Original Intent,* penned by the author of this work. Both are available from WallBuilders through the online store at www.wallbuilders.com or by calling 1-800-873-2845.

Franklin – one of America's least religious Founding Fathers – was a strong advocate of teaching Christian principles in public education.

If there is any famous American from the Founding Era considered less religious than Benjamin Franklin, it certainly is Thomas Paine; yet it is striking to see what even Thomas Paine believed should be taught in public education. For example, in a lecture in Paris in 1797, Paine attacked the French public school system because of the secular anti-religious manner in which it taught science. Paine protested:

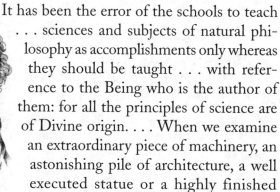

THOMAS PAINE

It has been the error of the schools to teach . . . sciences and subjects of natural philosophy as accomplishments only whereas they should be taught . . . with reference to the Being who is the author of them: for all the principles of science are of Divine origin. . . . When we examine an extraordinary piece of machinery, an astonishing pile of architecture, a well executed statue or a highly finished painting . . . our ideas are naturally led to think of the extensive genius and talents of the artist. When we study the elements of geometry, we think of Euclid. When we speak of gravitation, we think of Newton. How then is it, that when we study the works of God in the creation, we stop short and do not think of God? It is from the error of the schools. . . .

[T]he evil that has resulted . . . has been that of generating in the pupils a species of atheism. Instead of looking through the works of the creation to the Creator Himself, they stop short and employ the knowledge they acquire to create doubts of His existence. [109]

Not even Thomas Paine – probably the least religious among the American Founders – believed that public education should be so secular as to exclude religious and moral teachings.

America's first colonial educational laws, its first federal laws, and the declarations of many early American statesmen confirm the fact that the unique American approach to a successful education integrated religious and moral lessons with academic instruction. Subsequent textbooks demonstrate that this philosophy of education remained intact and unaltered for centuries.

FAMOUS AMERICAN TEXTBOOKS AND EDUCATORS

The *McGuffey Readers* were written in the 1830s-40s by William Holmes McGuffey, a noted university president and professor. His *Readers* became some of the most popular textbooks in the history of American education, selling over 122 million copies in their first 75 years of use [110] (fortunately, his *Readers* are still available for use in schools today [111]). So profound was McGuffey's influence on American public education that he has been titled "The Schoolmaster of the Nation."

WILLIAM HOLMES MCGUFFEY

His *Readers* introduced students to an anthology of some of the best literature in the English language. In the preface to his *Third Reader*, McGuffey (speaking in the third person) acknowledged the sources from which he had chosen those noteworthy pieces:

> In making his selections . . . the author has drawn from the purest fountains of English literature and aimed to combine simplicity with sense, elegance with simplicity, and piety with both. . . . For the copious extracts made from the

Sacred Scriptures, he makes no apology. Indeed, upon a review of the work, he is not sure but an apology may be due for his not having still more liberally transferred to its pages the chaste simplicity, the thrilling pathos, the living descriptions, and the matchless sublimity of the Sacred Writings. [112]

Similar acknowledgments about his reliance on the Scriptures can also be found in other of his *Readers*. [113] It is therefore not surprising that those famous *Readers* contained selections from the Scriptures as well as lessons bearing titles such as "The Character of Jesus Christ," "The Golden Rule," "Extract from the Sermon on the Mount," "Solomon's Wise Choice," "The Goodness of God," "Gospel Invitation," "Christian Light and Hope," "Consolation of Religion to the Poor," "Awake Zion," "On Prayer," and similarly strong religious pieces among the literary works. In fact, the McGuffey texts even had lessons on the Ten Commandments. [114]

THE TEN COMMANDMENTS

I am the Lord thy God

Thou shalt have no other gods before me

Thou shalt not make unto thee any graven image

Thou shalt not take the name of the Lord thy God in vain

Remember the Sabbath day to keep it holy

Honor thy father and thy mother

Thou shalt not kill

Thou shalt not commit adultery

Thou shalt not steal

Thou shalt not bear false witness

Thou shalt not covet

(Significantly, three of the most widely-used texts in America's educational history – *The New England Primers*, the Webster textbooks, [115] and the *McGuffey Readers* – all taught the Ten Commandments to students in public schools.)

Another famous educator was Emma Willard, † a pioneer in education for women. She championed academic (rather than just domestic) education and started schools for women in which subjects such as math and

---

† Emma Willard is one of the three faces depicted on the cover of this booklet, the center of the three individuals.

philosophy were taught – academic subjects never before taught to women in American education. [116] Willard also authored a number of textbooks; and like other successful American educators, she included religious and moral lessons within the framework of academic instruction.

In her famous textbook, *A System of Universal History*, she begins the study of world history with the Biblical account of creation. The progress of world history following creation is then simply a recounting of Biblical history, including lessons on "The Deluge" (the flood), "The Tower of Babel," "Babylon founded," "Nineveh built," "Calling of Abraham," "Sodom destroyed," "Joseph sold," "Jacob goes down to Egypt," "Moses born," etc. [117]

African American education was another emerging area of American education in the 1800s, and John Chavis was a famous black American educator of that period. Although he grew up in a segregated America, he nevertheless studied in higher education at the prominent colleges of Princeton in New Jersey, and Washington (now called Washington & Lee) in Virginia. As a black American in the 1830s, he broke through many walls of North Carolina segregation and not only preached to white congregations but he also educated both white and black students in his school; and many of his students went on to become governors, senators, and other influential leaders. [118] John Chavis taught his students a rigorous academic program and like all

JOHN CHAVIS

other successful American educators of any race or gender, he never divorced religious and moral lessons from academic instruction. [119]

Booker T. Washington [†] was another famous African American educator – one of the most significant of all black educators. Not only did he head the famous Tuskegee Institute but he also started a Bible college to improve education for Gospel ministers in black churches. [120] His students from Tuskegee became leaders and educators across the nation. Washington's own practice was to spend time in the Bible

BOOKER T. WASHINGTON

every day, [121] and he incorporated religious exercises into the academic studies at Tuskegee. In fact, Tuskegee students not only received religious and moral lessons during the course of their regular academic studies but they were also required to attend chapel services, where Booker T. himself delivered lessons and sermons. [122]

STUDENTS AT TUSKEGEE   CHAPEL AT TUSKEGEE

Since schools for black as well as white students, female as well as male students, included religious and moral lessons as part of the academic instruction, it is not surprising that the schools that opened their doors to all students without regard to race or gender also included religious and moral lessons in their academics.

One such excellent example was Oberlin College in Ohio. Founded in 1833, the Rev. Charles Finney (a prominent minister during the Second Great Awakening) was perhaps its most famous president. Oberlin was one of the first colleges in America to admit men and women, blacks and whites, as equals. That school had a profound

† Booker T. Washington is depicted on the front cover of this booklet, the right of the three individuals.

impact on American education and culture: many of its students became some of the most effective conductors on the Underground Railroad, guiding escaping slaves from the South to freedom in the North; and its students were instrumental in founding a number of famous universities, including several black universities. [123]

The academic program at Oberlin was rigorous and included religious and moral instruction. In fact, Finney boldly declared to all students:

> A good education is indeed a great good; but if not sanctified, it is . . . odious to God. . . . Th[e] very acquisitions [of education that] will give you higher esteem among men will, if unsanctified, make your character more utterly odious before God. You are a polished writer and a beautiful speaker! – You stand at the head of the college in these important respects! –Your friends look forward with hopeful interest to the time when you will be heard of on the floors of Senates, moving them to admiration by your eloquence! But alas, you have no piety! [124]

REV. CHARLES FINNEY

Daniel Webster was another famous American who had a direct influence both on American education and on its educational institutions. Webster served three decades in Congress, was Secretary of State for three different Presidents, and personally argued and won numerous cases before the U. S. Supreme Court.

One such case dealt with a public school in Philadelphia that forbade any minister on campus. [125] It was believed that this provision was an attempt to prevent religious instruction at the school. (Significantly, attorneys on both sides of the case found that anti-religious provision to be odious. [126])

DANIEL WEBSTER

THE U. S. SUPREME COURT

MR. WEBSTER'S SPEECH

IN DEFENCE OF

THE CHRISTIAN MINISTRY,

AND IN FAVOR OF THE

RELIGIOUS INSTRUCTION OF THE YOUNG.

DELIVERED IN THE

SUPREME COURT OF THE UNITED STATES,

FEBRUARY 10, 1844,

IN THE CASE OF STEPHEN GIRARD'S WILL.

WASHINGTON:
PRINTED BY GALES AND SEATON.
1844.

At the Court, what from others might have been nothing more than a dry legal argument, from Webster's lips became an emotional appeal on the importance of preserving religious instruction at the school. His argument before the Court lasted three days, and on the third day, Webster's argument was taken almost completely from the Bible. (His argument from that day was quickly published and distributed across the nation under the title *Mr. Webster's Speech in Defence of the Christian Ministry and in Favor of the Religious Instruction of the Young, Delivered in the Supreme Court of the United States on February 10, 1844.* [127]) In his argument, Webster reminded the Court:

When little children were brought into the presence of the Son of God, His disciples proposed to send them away, but [Jesus] said, "Suffer little children to come unto Me" [MATTHEW 19:14]. Unto Me! .... And that injunction is of perpetual obligation; it addresses itself today with the same earnestness and the same authority which attended its first utterance to the Christian world. It is of force everywhere and at all times; it extends to the ends of the earth, it will reach to the end of time always and everywhere sounding in the ears of men with an . . . authority which nothing can supersede. "Suffer little children to come unto Me." [128]

He opposed any plan of education that excluded religious instruction – any plan that forbade children to "come unto Him" at school.

How did the Court rule in that case? In a unanimous decision written by famous Justice Joseph Story (a "Father of American Jurisprudence" and placed on the Court under President James Madison), the Supreme Court declared:

> Why may not the Bible, and especially the New Testament, without note or comment, be read and taught as a Divine revelation in the [school] – its general precepts expounded . . . and its glorious principles of morality inculcated? . . . Where can the purest principles of morality be learned so clearly or so perfectly as from the New Testament? [129]

JUSTICE JOSEPH STORY

In the 19th century, the U.S. Supreme Court was still protecting the philosophy of education that had been introduced into America over two centuries earlier. And strikingly, more than a century after that case (in the 1950s), the Supreme Court continued to maintain a similar position toward religious instruction in schools, declaring:

> When the State encourages religious instruction, or cooperates with religious authorities by adjusting the schedule of public events to sectarian needs, it follows the best of our traditions. For it then respects the religious nature of our people and accommodates the public service to their spiritual needs. To hold that it may not would be to find in the Constitution a requirement that the government show a callous indifference to religious groups. That would be preferring those who believe in no religion over those who do believe. . . . [W]e find no [such] constitutional requirement. [130]

This was the position of the Supreme Court – and of early text-books and educators – on the issue of religious instruction in public schools over halfway through the 20th century. This was not surprising, however, for it was the same position that had been maintained throughout American education in four consecutive centuries.

MEASURING THE RESULTS OF EDUCATIONAL PHILOSOPHIES

Much clear and unequivocal evidence has been presented to demonstrate that the inclusion of religious and moral lessons was the accepted norm for four centuries in America. American educational philosophy mirrored the philosophy set forth long before by reformer Martin Luther, whose influence on public education was substantial. In fact, much of the emphasis on education so apparent among America's early settlers had come from the teachings and example of Martin Luther, who had advocated and encouraged the formation of public schools in Europe to help eliminate the illiteracy that had both characterized and perpetuated the Dark Ages. [131]

EDUCATOR MARTIN LUTHER

The educational philosophy of world renowned educator Martin Luther had been clear – and it was the same philosophy embraced in American education for centuries:

> I would advise no one to send his child where the Holy Scriptures are not supreme. Every institution that does not unceasingly pursue the study of God's Word becomes corrupt. . . . I greatly fear that the [schools], unless they teach the Holy Scriptures diligently and impress them on the young students, are wide gates to Hell. [132]

For centuries, American education included religious and moral principles as part of student instruction – and there is no question of the academic success of that philosophy. However, there have been great changes in recent years. Beginning in 1962, the courts ordered a completely secular approach to public education:

- Voluntary prayer was forbidden; [133]
- The inclusion of Scripture was terminated; [134]
- Elective classes on religion were halted; [135]
- The Bible was ordered out of school libraries; [136]
- Ten Commandments displays were ordered removed; [137]
- Religious artwork was covered; [138]
- Religious content in student papers and speeches was forbidden and even penalized, [139] with students being given a zero if they wrote on a religious topic; [140]
- Invocations were excluded from graduations and athletic events; [141]
- Students were disciplined for bringing their personal Bibles to read during free reading time; [142]
- Traditional Christmas programs were halted [143] as was the practice of students giving Christmas cards. [144]
- The names of previously celebrated holidays (e.g., Christmas, Thanksgiving, Easter, etc.) were changed to become completely secular (Fall Break, Winter Break, Spring Break).

There are literally scores of other similar rulings and policies that have established public education as an aggressively secular principality.

Significantly, following the implementation of a new educational paradigm based on the official exclusion of basic religious and moral principles in 1962, educational scores plummeted [†] – evidenced by the dramatic decline in college-bound student SAT scores. [145] Furthermore, in numerous recent international academic competitions, American high school students regularly finish last, near the last, or in the bottom half of students in math and

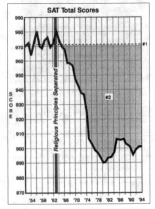

† Other charts amplifying the decline may be found in the book *America: to Pray or Not to Pray*, available from the online store at www.wallbuilders.com or by calling 1-800-873-2845.

science testing. [146] In fact, one recent international testing found that although American elementary students performed _above_ average, junior high students performed only _at_ average and American high school students finished at the bottom – well _below_ average. [147] This sequence of results prompted one critic to remark: "The longer U. S. students stay in school, the less they seem to know." [148]

Another indicator of the current unsatisfactory results is the fact that illiteracy has skyrocketed. America now ranks a dismal 65th in the world in literacy among its 200 nations, and a number of third-world nations currently post higher literacy rates than the United States; [149] yet only a few decades ago America had one of the world's highest literacy rates. Illiteracy is now so rampant that among recent high school graduates, 700,000 of them – after twelve years of public school – were unable to read their own diplomas! [150]

These are not the educational results that Americans had experienced under the former philosophy of education. In fact, the marked and visible deterioration in the quality of public education has produced a rapid rise in the popularity of and support for school choice: almost two dozen States have now passed some form of educational reforms to give students and their parents an opportunity to escape failing public school systems. [151]

It is irrefutable that the educational achievements of earlier generations stand in stark contrast to those of today; this can be shown not only statistically but also anecdotally, for numerous students in previous years routinely achieved at an early age what today we would consider extraordinary. For example:

- Declaration signer Charles Carroll entered college at the age of 10. [152]
- Fisher Ames entered Harvard when he was twelve. [153]
- Benjamin Rush graduated from Princeton when he was fourteen. [154]

CHARLES CARROLL

- John Trumbull – a law student under John Adams and a justice on the Supreme Court of Connecticut – had already read through the Bible for the first time when he was four years old; when he was seven-and-a-half years old, he passed the entrance exam to Yale University (however, since many American students began college at the age of thirteen or fourteen, his parents decided to hold him out until he was thirteen so that he could attend college with his peers.) [155]

There are many similar examples; and while entering a university at the age of thirteen or fourteen seems amazing to us today, it was not at that time – and the academics then were much more rigorous than they are today. Consider some additional examples of how our earlier educational system equipped young Americans for great achievements:

- Andrew Jackson (who later became a U. S. President) was serving as a soldier in the American Revolution when only fourteen years old; he was captured and made a prisoner of war by the British. [156]

- When John Quincy Adams was eight years old, he performed musket drills during the Revolution with the famous Massachusetts Minutemen; [157] when he was eleven, he received a congressional diplomatic appointment overseas as Secretary to the Ambassador in Paris and at the age of fourteen received a similar appointment to the Court of Catherine the Great in Russia. [158]

JOHN QUINCY ADAMS

- When Constitution signer William Livingston was fourteen, he moved in among the Mohawk Indians to live as a missionary. [159]

WILLIAM LIVINGSTON

- James Iredell – a Justice placed on the Supreme Court by George Washington – was appointed to public office in North Carolina to oversee financial matters when he was just seventeen years old. [160]

JAMES IREDELL

Such examples are almost unimaginable today, but these accounts simply were not that unusual under the American educational system at that time.

If critics believe that the above anecdotes represent only a few selected examples – that is, they represent the exceptions rather than the rule – then review the questions on p. 3 from the 1862 fourth grade geography test; how many fourth grade students today (or even adults) could pass that test? Or answer the elementary mental math questions from 1877 – or the history questions from 1882. Or for that matter, simply surf the web for the eighth grade exit tests used in most States around 1890 and then have students today (or even adults) try taking those tests.

And remember *Webster's Blue Back Speller*? Contemplate some of the spelling words that were taught in <u>elementary</u> schools for 150 years: "contumelious," "ichthyology," "bronchotomy," "loquacious," "mendacity," "armigerous," "vertiginous," "oleaginous," "acanthus" [161] – and there are many other words in this "elementary" spelling book that most Americans today have probably never seen.

| THE
ELEMENTARY
SPELLING BOOK,
BEING
AN IMPROVEMENT
ON THE
AMERICAN SPELLING BOOK.

BY NOAH WEBSTER, LL.D. | *Spelling Book.* 131
book, dŏve, fŭll, use, ean, chaise, gĕm, thin, thou.

Words of five syllables, accented on the fourth.
An ti seor bu' tie   gen e a loġ ie
ar is to erat' ie   lex i eo graph ie
char ae ter is tie   mon o syl lab ie
ee ele si as tie   or ni tho loġ ie
en thu si as tie   os te o loġ ie
en to mo loġ ie   phys i o loġ ie
ep i gram mat ie   ieh thy o loġ ie |

Considering the academic proficiency of previous generations, it appears that the American system of education received the benefit of the Scriptural promise in Proverbs 1:7: "The fear of the Lord is the beginning of <u>knowledge</u>."

It would not have surprised Dr. Benjamin Rush to learn that our academic achievements have fallen significantly since the secularization of public education, for he had long ago observed:

> [T]here is the most knowledge in those countries where there is the most Christianity. . . . [and] those . . . parents or school-masters who neglect the religious instruction of their children and

DR. BENJAMIN RUSH

pupils, reject and neglect the most effectual means of promoting <u>knowledge</u> in our country. [162] (emphasis added)

The successful philosophy of education that characterized America for centuries clearly has undergone a radical revolution in recent years; yet it is a revolution caused not by citizen action or legislative interference but rather by judicial activism, with courts and judges suddenly prohibiting what had been permissible for centuries. Secularization of education is the new paradigm; but recent decades clearly demonstrate that the more secular education becomes, the less successful it is academically.

Apparently, many today are unaware of the massive and dramatic changes that have occurred in American education in recent decades; and too many others are simply complacent about the changes. Yet, it is important that every citizen today – regardless of whether they have students in school – be concerned and informed about the condition of education. As educator Noah Webster long ago warned:

> The education of youth should be watched with the most scrupulous attention. . . . [I]t is much easier to introduce and establish an effectual system . . . than to correct by penal

NOAH WEBSTER

statutes the ill effects of a bad system. . . . The education of youth . . . lays the foundations on which both law and gospel rest for success. [161]

Every citizen should exert the time and effort necessary to ensure that schools are teaching sound content and providing a good education, and that those who teach in the classrooms – as well as those elected to school boards and legislatures – are individuals who respect, honor, and embrace the time-tested principles of a sound education. And if the leaders and schools you work with do not embrace these ideals, then replace the leaders – or start new schools.

Imparting mere academic knowledge should never be a sufficient final objective for learning, nor should the secularization of education ever become acceptable. A sound education should instill the three elements long proven to be the basis of a successful education: religion, morality, and knowledge. (These elements should be instilled not only in our schools but also in our homes, churches, and throughout our communities.)

For four centuries in American education, the three essential elements of religion, morality, and knowledge formed the basis of character and achievement; experience and common sense demonstrate that these elements still provide the foundation that will enable today's students to be the solid citizens and the great leaders of the future. It is our responsibility as citizens not only to protect the proven educational philosophy that made and has kept America great but also to do everything that we can to transmit that successful educational philosophy to future generations, just as our forebears did throughout the first four centuries of American education. ■

Endnotes

1. From an original in our possession, entitled Fourth Grade Questions: Geography, Chicago, March 27, 1862.

2. Joseph Ray, M. D., *Three Thousand Test Examples in Arithmetic: Drill Exercises for Review* (Cincinnati: Sargeant, Wilson & Hinkle, 1862), pp. 94, 95, "Articles 215 & 217. – Stocks," #4 & #5.

3. *Ray's New Intellectual Arithmetic* (Cincinnati: Van Antwerp, Bragg & Co., 1877), p. 114, "Article 217. – Stocks," #4, p. 114, "Lesson LXI," #13 & #16.

4. *Ray's New Intellectual Arithmetic*, p. 115, Lesson LXII, #16.

5. B. A. Hathaway, *1001 Questions and Answers on United States History; Including the Constitution and Amendments* (Cleveland: The Burrows Brothers Company, 1882), p. 92, "The Constitution," #90-94.

6. Alexander Hamilton, John Jay, and James Madison, *The Federalist, on the New Constitution Written in 1788* (Philadelphia: Benjamin Warner, 1818).

7. Professor Dr. John Eidsmoe at the Jones School of Law, at the time of this writing, serving at Faulkner University, in Birmingham, Alabama. Dr. Eidsmoe holds multiple doctorates and masters degrees and has taught at several law schools, including Coburn School of Law in Tulsa, Oklahoma, and Regent School of Law in Virginia Beach, Virginia.

8. *Quinquennial Catalogue of the Officers and Graduates of Harvard University, 1636–1895* (Cambridge, MA: Harvard University, 1895), Index of Graduates, pp. 421, 422, 442, 447, 454, 458, 463, 467, 469, 484, 487, 512.

9. *The Harvard Graduates' Magazine* (Manesh, WI: George Barna Publishing Co.), September 1933, p. 8, from the article "Harvard Seals and Arms" by Samuel Eliot Morison. English translation also confirmed to the author in an October 18, 1995, letter from a curatorial associate at the Harvard University Archives.

10. Benjamin Pierce, *A History of Harvard University* (Cambridge, MA: Brown, Shattuck, and Company, 1833), Appendix, p. 5.

11. Pierce, *A History of Harvard University*, Appendix, p. 5.

12. Henry P. Johnston, *Yale and Her Honor-Roll in the American Revolution, 1775-1783* (New York: Privately published, 1888), pp. 5-7; *Dictionary of American Biography*, Dumas Malone, editor (New York: Charles Scribner's Sons, 1936), s.v. "Webster, Noah"; "Wolcott, Oliver"; "Ingersoll, Jared"; "Swift, Zephaniah"; "Kent, James."

13. *The Catalogue of the Library of Yale College in New Haven* (New London: T. Green, 1743), prefatory remarks; see also *The Catalogue of the Library of Yale College in New Haven* (New Haven: James Parker, 1755), prefatory remarks.

14. *The Laws of Yale College in New Haven in Connecticut* (New Haven: Josiah Meigs, 1787), pp. 5-6, Chapter II, Article 1, 4.

15. Samuel Davies Alexander, *Princeton College During the Eighteenth Century* (Anson D. F. Randolph & Company, 1872), pp. 2, 66, 86, 106, 139, 143, 148, 165, 194.

16. Thomas Jefferson Wertenbaker, *Princeton: 1746-1896* (Princeton: Princeton University Press, 1946), p. 88; Lawrence A. Cremin, *American Education: The Colonial Experience, 1607-1783* (New York, Evanston, and London: Harper & Row, 1970), p. 301; *Nation Under God: A Religious-Patriotic Anthology*, Frances Brentano, editor (Great Neck, NY: Channel Press, 1957), pp. 41-42; Dr. John Eidsmoe, *Christianity and The Constitu-*

tion (Grand Rapids: Baker Books, 1987), p. 83; Alexander, *Princeton College During the Eighteenth Century*, pp. 121-185.

17. *The Laws of the College of New-Jersey* (Trenton: Isaac Collins, 1794), p. 5.

18. John Witherspoon, *The Works of the Reverend John Witherspoon* (Philadelphia: William W. Woodward, 1802), Vol. III, p. 42, from "The Dominion of Providence over the Passions of Men," delivered at Princeton on May 17, 1776.

19. Elias Boudinot, *An Oration Delivered at Elizabeth-Town, New-Jersey, Agreeably to a Resolution of the State Society of Cincinnati, on the Fourth of July, 1793* (Elizabeth-Town: Shepard Kollock, 1793), p. 14.

20. William V. Wells, *The Life and Public Service of Samuel Adams* (Boston: Little, Brown, & Co., 1865), Vol. I, p. 22, quoting from a political essay by Samuel Adams published in The Public Advertiser, 1749.

21. Fisher Ames, *An Oration on the Sublime Virtues of General George Washington* (Boston: Young & Minns, 1800), p. 23.

22. Bernard C. Steiner, *The Life and Correspondence of James McHenry* (Cleveland: The Burrows Brothers, 1907), p. 475; in a letter from Charles Carroll to James McHenry of November 4, 1800.

23. George Washington, *Address of George Washington, President of the United States, and Late Commander in Chief of the American Army, to the People of the United States, Preparatory to his Declination* (Baltimore: Christopher Jackson, 1796), pp. 22-23.

24. Varnum Lansing Collins, *President Witherspoon, a Biography* (Princeton: Princeton University Press, 1925), Vol. II, p. 217.

25. Helen Chavis Othow, *John Chavis: African American Patriot, Preacher, Teacher, and Mentor (1763-1838)* (Jefferson, NC: McFarland & Company, Inc., 2001), pp. 41, 43, 90, 111; see also Collins, *President Witherspoon*, Vol. II, p. 217.

26. See, for example, Benjamin Franklin, *The Papers of Benjamin Franklin*, William B. Willcox, editor (New Haven: Yale University Press, 1972), Vol. 15, p. 30, letter from Benjamin Franklin to Francis Hopkinson on January 24, 1768, and Vol. 14, p. 340, letter from Benjamin Franklin to Francis Hopkinson on December 16, 1767.

27. See, for example, Franklin, *The Papers of Benjamin Franklin*, Vol. 7, pp. 100-101, letter from John Waring to Benjamin Franklin on January 24, 1757; p. 356, letter from Benjamin Franklin to John Waring on January 3, 1758; pp. 377-378, letter from Benjamin Franklin to John Waring on February 17, 1758; Vol. 9, pp. 12-13, letter from John Waring to Benjamin Franklin on January 4, 1760, also n1; pp. 20-21, "Minutes of the Associates of the Late Dr. Bray" on January 17, 1760; pp. 298-300, letter from Benjamin Franklin to John Waring on June 27, 1763; pp. 395-396, letter from Benjamin Franklin to John Waring on December 17, 1763; Vol. 13, p. 442, letter from Benjamin Franklin to Abbot Upcher on October 4, 1766; and others.

28. See for example Benjamin Rush's January 14, 1795 letter to the Pennsylvania Abolition Society. Benjamin Rush, *Letters of Benjamin Rush*, L. H. Butterfield, editor (Princeton: Princeton University Press, 1951), Vol. II, pp. 757-758.

29. Benjamin Rush, *Essays, Literary, Moral and Philosophical* (Philadelphia: Thomas and Samuel F. Bradford, 1798), pp. 75-92, "Thoughts upon Female Education, Accommodated to the Present State of Society, Manners, and Government, in the United States of America. Addressed to the Visitors of the Young Ladies' Academy in Philadelphia, 28th July, 1787, at the Close of the Quarterly Examination, and Afterwards Published at the Request of the Visitors."

30. The Nuremberg Project, "July 6, 1945 - The Nazi Master Plan: The Persecution of the Christian Churches" (at http://www.camlaw.rutgers.edu/publications/law-religion/

nuremberg/nurinst1.htm); see also *Christianity Today*, "Christian History Corner: Final Solution, Part II" (at http://www.christianitytoday.com/ct/2002/102/52.0.html), and BBC News, "Nazi trial documents made public" (at http://news.bbc.co.uk/1/hi/world/americas/1753469.stm).

31. While Hitler had 6 million Jews murdered, he was responsible for the deaths of a total of 20.9 million people. See Holocaust Encyclopedia, "The Holocaust" (at http://www.ushmm.org/wlc/en/index.php?lang=en&ModuleId=10005143), and R. J. Rummel, *Death By Government* (New Brunswick: Transaction Publishers, 1994), p. 8.

32. See for example, The History Channel, "In Search of History: Hitler and the Occult" (at http://store.aetv.com/html/product/index.jhtml?id=72289&browseCategoryId=&location=&parentcatid=&subcatid=), and the list of books at Brough's Books, "Nazi Occultism" (at http://www.dropbears.com/b/broughsbooks/military/occult_nazism.htm).

33. R. J. Rummel, *Death By Government* (New Brunswick: Transaction Publishers, 1994), p. 4.

34. Rummel, *Death*, p. 8.

35. Daniel Dorchester, *Christianity in the United States* (New York: Hunt and Eaton, 1890), p. 124.

36. A total of 22 people were murdered in these three incidents. See CNN.com, "Are U.S. Schools Safe?" (at http://www.cnn.com/SPECIALS/1998/schools/), and "Third student dies in Kentucky school shooting" (at http://www.cnn.com/US/9712/02/school.shooting.on/); PBS, "Online News Hour: Church Shooting" (at http://www.pbs.org/newshour/bb/law/july-dec99/shooting_9-16a.html).

37. William Warren Sweet, *The Story of Religion in America* (New York: Harper & Brothers, 1950), p. 61; quoted in Peter Marshall and David Manuel, *The Light and the Glory* (Grand Rapids: Fleming H. Revell, 1977), p. 238.

38. *Dictionary of American Biography*, s.v. "Mather, Increase" and "Brattle, Thomas"; Court TV's Crime Library, "The Salem Witch Trials: Reason Returns" (at http://www.crimelibrary.com/notorious_murders/not_guilty/salem_witches/12.html?sect=12).

39. John Witherspoon, *The Works of John Witherspoon* (1815), Vol. V, pp. 325-326, "The Trial of Religious Truth by Its Moral Influence," October 9, 1759.

40. Benjamin Franklin, *The Works of Benjamin Franklin*, Jared Sparks, editor (Boston: Tappan, Whittemore and Mason, 1840), Vol. X, p. 282, to Thomas Paine.

41. *The Code of 1650, Being a Compilation of the Earliest Laws and Orders of the General Court of Connecticut* (Hartford: Silus Andrus, 1822), pp. 90-92; see also *Church of the Holy Trinity v. U. S.*, 143 U. S. 457, 467 (1892).

42. Edward Kendall, *Travels through the Northern Parts of the United States, in the Years 1807 and 1808* (New York: I. Riley, 1809).

43. Kendall, *Travels*, Vol. I, pp. 270-271.

44. Alexis de Tocqueville, *The Republic of the United States of America and Its Political Institutions, Reviewed and Examined,* Henry Reeves, translator (Garden City, NY: A. S. Barnes & Co., 1851).

45 There are numerous editions of this work in print, both abridged (such as Alexis de Tocqueville, *Democracy in America: Specially Edited and Abridged for the Modern Reader*, Richard D. Heffner, editor (New York: Penguin Books, 1984)), and unabridged (such as Alexis de Tocqueville, *Democracy in America*, translated by George Lawrence, edited by J. P. Mayer, (New York: Doubleday & Company, Inc., 1969)).

46. See, for example, 1969 translation by Lawrence, pp. 45, 302, 590.

47. *United States Code Annotated* (St. Paul: West Publishing Co., 1987), "The Organic Laws of the United States of America," p. 1. This work lists America's four fundamental laws as the Articles of Confederation, the Declaration of Independence, the Constitution, and the Northwest Ordinance.

48. *The Constitutions of the United States of America With the Latest Amendments* (Trenton: Moore and Lake, 1813), p. 364, "An Ordinance of the Territory of the United States Northwest of the River Ohio," Article III.

49. *Constitutions* (1813), p. 364, "An Ordinance of the Territory of the United States Northwest of the River Ohio," Article III. 2-79. Acts Passed at a Congress . . . in the Year 1789, pp. 178-179, May 26, 1790; see also *Laws of Arkansas Territory*, Compiled and Arranged . . . Under the Direction and Superintendance of John Pope, Esq., Governor of the Territory of Arkansas (Little Rock, Ark. Ter.: J. Steele, Esq., 1835), p. 31, "Organic Law. Chapter I, § 14."

50. *Constitutions* (1813), p. 334, Ohio, 1802, Article 8, § 3.

51. *The Constitutions of All the United States According to the Latest Amendments* (Lexington, KY: Thomas T. Skillman, 1817), p. 389, Mississippi, 1817, Article 9, § 16.

52. House of Representatives, Mis. Doc. No. 44, 35th Congress, 2nd Session, February 2, 1859, pp. 3-4, Article 1, § 7, of the Kansas Constitution.

53. M. B. C. True, *A Manual of the History and Civil Government of the State of Nebraska* (Omaha: Gibson, Miller, & Richardson, 1885), p. 34, Nebraska, 1875, Article 1, § 4.

54. See, for example, *The Constitution of North Carolina* (Raleigh: Rufus L. Edmisten, 1989), p. 42, Article 9, § 1; *Constitution of the State of Nebraska* (Lincoln: Allen J. Beermann, 1992), pp. 1-2, Article 1, § 4; *Page's Ohio Revised Code Annotated* (Cincinnati: Anderson Publishing Co., 1994), p. 24, Article 1, § 7; *The Constitution of Michigan*, Article VIII, §1.

55. *Columbia History of Education in Kansas*, Complied by Kansas Educators (Topeka: Edwin H. Snow, 1893).

56. *Columbia History of Education in Kansas*, p. 81.

57. *Columbia History of Education in Kansas*, p. 81.

58. *Columbia History of Education in Kansas*, p. 82.

59. *Bible Study Course, New Testament;* The Dallas High Schools, Bulletin No. 170, Authorized by the Board of Education, April 23, 1946 (Dallas, TX: Dallas Public Schools' Print Shop, 1946), p. 5.

60. *Bible Study Course, New Testament; The Dallas High Schools*, pp. 5-6.

61. Warren A. Nord, *Religion & American Education* (The University of North Carolina Press, 1995), p. 84, quoting from James Tunstead Burtchaell, "The Decline and Fall of the Christian College I," First Things, May 1991, p. 24, and George Marsden, *The Soul of the American University* (New York: Oxford University Press, 1992), p. 11.

62. Nord, *Religion & American Education*, p. 84, and Marsden, *The Soul of the American University*, p. 11.

63. See, for example, *Samuel Adams and John Adams, Four Letters: Being an Interesting Correspondence Between Those Eminently Distinguished Characters, John Adams, Late President of the United States; and Samuel Adams, Late Governor of Massachusetts. On the Important Subject of Government* (Boston: Adams and Rhoades, 1802); George Washington, *Address of George Washington. . . Preparatory to his Declination* (Baltimore: Christopher Jackson, 1796), pp. 23-24; Benjamin Rush, *Letters of Benjamin Rush*, L. H. Butterfield, editor (Princeton: Princeton University Press, 1951), Vol. 1, pp. 388-389, letter from Benjamin Rush to Richard Price on May 25, 1786; Noah Webster, *History of the United States* (New-Haven: Durrie & Peck, 1832), p. 6.

64. *Dictionary of American Biography*, s.v. "Baldwin, Abraham"; "Webster, Noah"; "Rush, Benjamin"; "Jefferson, Thomas"; "Franklin, Benjamin"; etc.

65. Benjamin Rush, *A Letter by Dr. Benjamin Rush Describing the Consecration of the German College at Lancaster* (Lancaster, PA: Published by Order of the College, 1945), pp. 9-10.

66. Dr. Benjamin Rush served as treasurer of the United States Mint from 1797-1813, serving under Presidents John Adams, Thomas Jefferson, and James Madison; see *Dictionary of American Biography*, s.v. "Rush, Benjamin."

67. The five included the College of Philadelphia, University of the State of Pennsylvania, Young Ladies' Academy of Philadelphia, Dickinson College, and Franklin College.

68. *Appletons' Cyclopaedia of American Biography* (New York: D. Appleton and Company, 1888) s.v. "Rush, Benjamin"; Benjamin Rush, *Essays, Literary, Moral and Philosophical* (Philadelphia: Thomas and Samuel F. Bradford, 1798), pp. 6-20, "Of the Mode of Education Proper in a Republic"; David Ramsay, *An Eulogium upon Benjamin Rush, M.D.* (Philadelphia: Bradford and Inskeep, 1813), p. 107.

69. Rush, *Essays*, pp. 93-94, "A Defense of the Use of the Bible as a School Book, Addressed to the Rev. Jeremy Belknap, of Boston," on March 10, 1791.

70. Rush, *Essays*, pp. 112-113, "A Defense of the Use of the Bible as a School Book, Addressed to the Rev. Jeremy Belknap, of Boston," on March 10, 1791.

71. Morris spoke 173 times on this floor – more than any others. U.S. National Archives & Records Administration, "The Founding Fathers: Gouverneur Morris, Pennsylvania" (at http://www.archives.gov/national_archives_experience/charters/constitution_founding_fathers_pennsylvania.html).

72. Continental Congress and Constitutional Convention: To Form a More Perfect Union (at http://memory.loc.gov/ammem/bdsds/constit.html); see also Philadelphia Daily News, July 3, 2003, William Bunch, "Test Your Constitutional Knowledge" (at http://www.philly.com/mld/dailynews/6224513.htm?1c).

73. Jared Sparks, *The Life of Gouverneur Morris, with Selections from His Correspondence and Miscellaneous Papers* (Boston: Gray & Bowen, 1832), Vol. III, p. 483, from his "Notes on the Form of a Constitution for France, September 14, 1791."

74. *The Debates and Proceedings in the Congress of the United States* (Washington, DC: Gales and Seaton, 1834), Vol. I, p. 796, September 24, 1789. See also Robert L. Cord, *Separation of Church and State: Historical Fact and Current Fiction* (Grand Rapids: Baker Book House, 1988), p. 8, and Daniel L. Dreisbach, *Real Threat and Mere Shadow: Religious Liberty and the First Amendment* (Westchester, IL: Crossway Books, 1987), p. 62.

75. Fisher Ames, *Notices of the Life and Character of Fisher Ames* (Boston: T. B. Wait & Co., 1809), p. 134.

76. Ames, *Notices*, pp. 134-135.

77. John Quincy Adams, *Letters of John Quincy Adams to His Son on the Bible and Its Teachings* (Auburn: James M. Alden, 1850), p. 34.

78 Henry Laurens, *The Papers of Henry Laurens*, George C. Rogers, Jr. and David R. Chesnutt, editors (Columbia, SC: University of South Carolina Press, 1980), Vol. VIII, pp. 426-427, from a letter to James Lawrenson on August 19, 1772.

79. Rush, *Essays*, pp. 94, 100, "A Defense of the Use of the Bible as a School Book."

80. *Roberts v. Madigan*, 702 F. Supp. 1505, 1506-1509 (D. Colo. 1989).

81. *Appletons' Cyclopaedia of American Biography*, s. v. "Webster, Noah"; Noah Webster, *An American Dictionary of the English Language* (Springfield, MA: George and Charles

Merriam, 1849), p. xvi, "Memoir of the Author"; The United States Constitution, Art. 1, § 8, Par. 8 (at http://www.house.gov/Constitution/Constitution.html).

82. W. S. Tyler, *History of Amherst College During Its First Half Century*. (Springfield, MA: Clark W. Bryan and Company. 1873) p. 104. See, for example, Noah Webster, *History of the United States* (New Haven: Durrie & Peck, 1832), *Elements of Useful Knowledge Containing a Historical and Geographical Account of the United States* (New-London: Ebenezer P. Cady, 1807), Vol. 1, *The Elementary Spelling Book* (Brattleborough, VT: 1823), *Value of the Bible, and Excellence of the Christian Religion* (New Haven: Durrie & Peck, 1834), *An American Selection of Lessons in Reading and Speaking* (Philadelphia: David Hogan, 1810), and *A Dictionary of the English Language* (New-York: White, Gallaher, & White, 1831).

83. H. R. Warfel, *Noah Webster, Schoolmaster to America* (New York: MacMillan Co, 1936); see also reprints of Webster's works such as William Webster, *A Sequel to Webster's Elementary Spelling Book* (Philadelphia: J. B. Lippincott Company, 1845).

84. Noah Webster, *The Elementary Spelling Book* (Wheeling, VA: James Stephenson, 1839).

85. Webster, *Elementary Spelling Book*, p. 168.

86. Noah Webster, *A Collection of Papers on Political, Literary, and Moral Subjects* (New York: Webster and Clark, 1843), p. 291, from his "Reply to a Letter of David McClure on the Subject of the Proper Course of Study in the Girard College, Philadelphia. New Haven, October 25, 1836."

87. See, for example, the fables, "The Boy Who Stole Apples," "The Cobler and his Son," "Honesty Rewarded," and "Agathocles and Calista," from Noah Webster, *American Selection of Lessons in Reading and Speaking* (Philadelphia: David Hogan, 1810), pp. 25-33.

88. Noah Webster, *History of the United States* (New Haven: Durrie & Peck, 1832), p. 6.

89. Webster, *History of the United States*, p. 339.

90. William Webster, *A Speller and Definer* (Philadelphia: J. B. Lippincott & Co., 1845), inside front cover.

91. *Dictionary of American Biography*, s. v., "Morse, Jedidiah."

92. Jedidiah Morse, *A Sermon, Exhibiting the Present Dangers and Consequent Duties of the Citizens of the United States of America. Delivered at Charlestown. April 25, 1799, The Day of the National Fast* (Hartford: Hudson and Goodwin, 1799), p. 9.

93. *A Compilation of the Messages and Papers of the Presidents*, James D. Richardson, editor (New York: Bureau of National Literature, 1897), Vol. I, pp. 194-195, from his "Eighth Annual Address," delivered on December 7, 1796.

94. George Washington, *The Writings of Washington*, John C. Fitzpatrick, editor (Washington, DC: US Government Printing Office, 1932), Vol. XV, p. 55, from his speech to the Delaware Indian Chiefs on May 12, 1779.

95. Washington, *Writings*, p. 55, from his speech to the Delaware Indian Chiefs on May 12, 1779.

96. William Wells, *The Life and Public Services of Samuel Adams* (Boston: Little, Brown, and Company, 1865), p. 412.

97. Samuel Adams and John Adams, *Four Letters*, pp. 9-10; see also, William V. Wells, *The Life and Public Services of Samuel Adams* (Boston, MA: Little, Brown and Company, 1865), Vol. III, p. 304.

98. Adams and Adams, *Four Letters*, p. 14; see also, Wells, *The Life and Public Services of Samuel Adams*, Vol. III, p. 304.

99. Paul Leicester Ford, *The New England Primer: A History of its Origin and Development* (New York: Dodd, Mead, and Co., 1897), plate xxiv, following p. 300.

100. *Dictionary of American History*, James Truslow Adams, editor (New York: Charles Scribner's Sons, 1940), s.v. "New-England Primer," p. 100.

101. Ford, *The New England Primer: A History*, pp. 16-19, 300; see also *The Columbia Encyclopedia* (at http://www.bartleby.com/65/ne/NewEngPrm.html); *The New England Primer: Twentieth Century Reprint* (Ginn & Company); *The New-England Primer* (Aledo, TX: Wallbuilder Press, 2003), and *The New-England Primer* (Vision Forum) (at http://www.visionforum.com/booksandtapes/productinfo.asp?number=12755&variation=&aitem=3&mitem=9&ref=booksandtapes%2Fproductlist%2Easp&refdept=4&refpn=), and *Webster's Blue-Backed Speller and New England Primer* (Hearthstone Publishing, 1999) (at http://www.amazon.com/exec/obidos/tg/detail/-/157558042X/002-2617697-5390462?v=glance)

102. *The New-England Primer* (Boston: Edward Draper, 1777), p. 8.

103. *The New-England Primer* (1777), p. 13.

104. *The New-England Primer* (1777), p. 49, "The Shorter Catechism."

105. Ford, *The New England Primer: A History*, pp. 310, 313.

106. See, for example, Franklin, *The Papers of Benjamin Franklin*, Vol. 7, pp. 100-101, letter from John Waring to Benjamin Franklin on January 24, 1757; p. 356, letter from Benjamin Franklin to John Waring on January 3, 1758; pp. 377-378, letter from Benjamin Franklin to John Waring on February 17, 1758; Vol. 9, pp. 12-13, letter from John Waring to Benjamin Franklin on January 4, 1760, also n1; pp. 20-21, "Minute of the Associates of the Late Dr. Bray" on January 17, 1760; Vol. 10, pp. 298-300, letter from Benjamin Franklin to John Waring on June 27, 1763; pp. 395-396, letter from Benjamin Franklin to John Waring on December 17, 1763; Vol. 13, p. 442, letter from Benjamin Franklin to Abbot Upcher on October 4, 1766; and others.

107. Benjamin Franklin, *Proposals Relating to the Education of Youth in Pennsylvania* (Philadelphia: University of Pennsylvania Press, 1931 reprint of 1749) p. vii, from the Introduction.

108. Franklin, *Proposals*, p. 22.

109. Thomas Paine, *Life and Writings of Thomas Paine*, Daniel Edwin Wheeler, editor (New York: Vincent Parke and Company, 1908), pp. 2-4, "The Study of God", delivered in Paris on January 16, 1797, in a Discourse to the Society of Theophilanthropists.

110. Houghton Mifflin Company, "McGuffey's Reader" (at http://college.hmco.com/history/readerscomp/rcah/html/ah_058200_mcguffeysrea.htm); see also Encyclopedia.com, "McGuffey, William Holmes" (at http://www.encyclopedia.com/html/m/mcg1uffey.asp); William H. McGuffey, *The First Reader For Young Children* (Cincinnati: Truman and Smith, 1983), Introduction.

111. Textbook.com, "The McGuffey Readers" (at http://www.textbookx.com/product_detail.php?affiliate=bizrate&detail_isbn=0312177666), and Amazon.com, "The McGuffey Readers" (at http://www.amazon.com/exec/obidos/ASIN/0312177666/bizrate-5k114-20/002-2617697-5390462).

112. William H. McGuffey, *Eclectic Third Reader* (Cincinnati: Winthrop B. Smith, 1853), Preface.

113. See for example: William H. McGuffey, *Eclectic Fourth Reader*, 1844 and 1849 editions, p. 9.

114. The Ten Commandments are found in the *McGuffey Second Reader*, Lesson LXIII (63), especially the editions from 1836-1853, and in the 1983 reprint.

115. See his *Advice to the Young*, reprinted by WallBuilders. The original content was printed in Noah Webster, *History of the United States*, (New-Haven: Durrie & Peck, 1832).

116. *Dictionary of American Biography*, s. v. "Willard, Emma Hart."

117. Emma Willard, *A System of Universal History in Perspective* (Hartford: F.J. Huntington, 1835).

118. G. C. Shaw, *John Chavis* (New York: Vail-Ballou Press, 1931) p. 24; Helen Chavis Othow, *John Chavis* (Jefferson, NC: McFarland & Company, Inc., 2001) p. 68.

119. *Dictionary of American Negro Biography*, s. v. "Chavis, John"; see also Shaw, *John Chavis*, pp.18, 21-22, 24; Othow, *John Chavis*, pp. 54-56, 63-66, 68, 70.

120. Booker T. Washington, *The Booker T. Washington Papers*, Louis R. Harlan, editor (Chicago: University of Illinois Press, 1972), Vol. 1, p. 382.

121. *Dictionary of American Biography*, s. v. "Washington, Booker Taliaferro."

122. *Dictionary of American Negro Biography*, Rayford Logan and Michael Winston, editors (New York: W.W. Norton & Company, 1982) s. v. "Washington, Booker T."

123. African American Registry, "Oberlin College founded" (at http://www.aaregistry.com/african_american_history/337/Oberlin_College_founded); Ohio History Central, "Oberlin College" (at http://www.ohiohistorycentral.org/ohc/history/ocoa/pla/obc.shtml); "The Town that Started the Civil War" (at http://history.sandiego.edu/gen/civilwar/04/oberlin.html).

124. Charles G. Finney, *Sermons on Gospel Themes* (New York: Fleming H. Revell Company, 1876), p. 358, "Men Often Highly Esteem What God Abhors."

125. *Vidal v. Girard's Executors*, 43 U. S. 126 (1844)

126. See *Vidal v. Girard's Executors*, 43 U. S. 126 (1844), wherein Webster's side called the clause "repugnant" (p. 143) and the other side called the clause "obnoxious" (p. 152).

127. Daniel Webster, *Mr. Webster's Speech in Defence of the Christian Ministry and in Favor of the Religious Instruction of the Youth. Delivered in the Supreme Court of the United States, February 10, 1844, in the Case of Stephen Girard's Will* (Washington, DC: Gales and Seaton, 1844), p. 27; see also Daniel Webster, *The Works of Daniel Webster* (Boston: Little, Brown, and Company, 1853), Vol. VI, pp. 153-154.

128. Webster, *Speech in Defence of the Christian Ministry*, p. 27; see also Webster, *Works*, Vol. VI, pp. 153-154.

129. *Vidal v. Girard's Executors*, 43 U. S. 126, 200 (1844).

130. *Zorach v. Clauson*, 343 U. S. 306, 313-314 (1952).

131. Encyclopedia Britannica, 11th edition (New York: Encyclopedia Britannica, Inc., 1911), s.v. "Luther, Martin"; Encyclopedia.com, "Luther, Martin (at http://www.encyclopedia.com/html/section/Luther-M_GrowthofLutheranismandHisLastYears.asp); New Advent, "Catholic Encyclopedia: Martin Luther" (at http://www.newadvent.org/cathen/09438b.htm).

132. Martin Luther, *Luther's Works: The Christian in Society*, James Atkinson, editor (Philadelphia: Fortress Press, 1966), Vol. 44, p. 207.

133. *Engel v. Vitale*, 370 U.S. 421 (1962). *Abington v. Schempp*, 374 U. S. 203 (1963). *Commissioner of Education v. School Committee of Leyden*, 267 N. E. 2d 226 (Sup. Ct. Mass. 1971), cert. denied, 404 U. S. 849.

134. *Abington v. Schempp*, 374 U. S. 203 (1963).

135. *McCollum v. Board of Education*, 333 U. S. 203, 207-209 (1948).

136. *Roberts v. Madigan*, 702 F. Supp. 1505 (D.C. Colo. 1989), 921 F. 2d 1047 (10 Cir. 1990), cert. denied, 112 S. Ct. 3025; 120 L. Ed. 2d 896.

137. *Stone v. Graham*, 449 U. S. 39 (1980). *Ring v. Grand Forks Public School District*, 483 F. Supp. 272 (D.C. ND 1980). *Lanner v. Wimmer*, 662 F. 2d 1349 (10th Cir. 1981).

138. *Washegesic v. Bloomingdale Public School*, 813 F. Supp. 559 (W.D. Mi., S.D. 1993); affirmed, 33 F. 3d 679 (6th Cir. 1994); cert. denied, 63 U.S.W.L. 3786 (May 1, 1995); cert. denied, *Fleming v. Jefferson County Sch. Dist.*, 298 F. 3d 918 (10th Cir. 2002).

139. *Stein v. Oshinsky*, 348 F. 2d 999 (2nd Cir. 1965), cert. denied, 382 U. S. 957. *Collins v. Chandler Unified School District*, 644 F. 2d 759 (9th Cir. 1981), cert. denied, 454 U. S. 863. *Bishop v. Aronov*, 926 F. 2d 1066 (11th Cir. 1991). *Duran v. Nitsche*, 780 F. Supp. 1048 (E.D. Pa. 1991).

140. *Brittney Kay Settle v. Dickson County School Board*, 53 F. 3d 152 (6th Cir. 1995), cert. denied, 64 L. W. 3478 (1995); see also *Dallas Morning News*, "Court rejects case of girl who wrote Jesus paper," November 28, 1995, p, 4-A; picked up on wire service from Los Angeles Times.

141. *Harris v. Joint School District* No. 241, 41 F. 3d 447 (9th Cir. 1994). *Gearon v. Loudoun County School Board*, 844 F. Supp. 1097 (U.S.D.C., E.D. Va. 1993). *Robert E. Lee v. Daniel Weisman*, 112 S. Ct. 2649; 120 L. Ed. 2d 467 (1992). *Kay v. Douglas School District*, 719 P. 2d 875 (Or. App. 1986). *Graham v. Central Community School District of Decatur County*, 608 F. Supp. 531 (U.S.D.C., Ia. 1985).

142. *Gierke v. Blotzer*, CV-88-0-883 (U.S.D.C. Neb. 1989).

143 *Florey v. Sioux Falls School District*, 464 F. Supp. 911 (U.S.D.C., SD 1979), cert. denied, 449 U. S. 987 (1980).

144. *The New American*, June 20, 1988, p. 19, "America Without God."

145. David Barton, *America: To Pray or Not to Pray?* (Aledo, TX: WallBuilder Press, 1994), pp. 57-62.

146. National Center for Educational Statistics, Department of Education, *The Condition of Education, 1987* (Washington, DC: US Government Printing Office, 1987), pp. 7-8.

147. National Center for Educational Statistics, Department of Education, "Highlights From TIMSS: Overview and Key Findings Across Grade Levels" (at http://nces.ed.gov/pubs99/1999081.pdf); see also The American School Board Journal, "Solving Problems in Math and Science Education" (at http://www.asbj.com/199807/0798coverstory.html); 4Choice, "International Test Scores" (at http://4brevard.com/choice/international-test-scores.htm), etc.

148. The American School Board Journal, "Solving Problems in Math and Science Education" (at http://www.asbj.com/199807/0798coverstory.html).

149. NationMaster.com, "Education: Literacy (total population)" (at http://www.nationmaster.com/graph-T/edu_lit_tot_pop&int=-1); see also Texas Literacy Council, Developing Human Capital, p. 2, 1991.

150. Statistics provided during a White House briefing attended by the author in September, 1989.

151. The Heritage Foundation, "Policy Research & Analysis: School Choice Programs in the States" (at http://www.heritage.org/Research/Education/Schools/schoolchoice_states.cfm).

152. Although there is some discrepancy regarding the exact age that Charles Carroll entered college, sources report his age as being between 8 and 11 years old. See, for example, *Dictionary of American Biography*, s.v. "Carroll, Charles"; USHistory.org, "Short Biographies on each of the 56 Declaration Signers" (at http://www.ushistory.org/declaration/signers/carroll.htm).

153. *Dictionary of American Biography*, s.v. "Ames, Fisher."

154. *Dictionary of American Biography*, s.v. "Rush, Benjamin."

155. Alexander Cowie, *John Trumbull: Connecticut Wit* (Chapel Hill: University of North Carolina Press, 1936), pp. 16-17, 20-21; see also, Edited Appleton's Encyclopedia, "Trumbull, John" (at http://famousamericans.net/johntrumbull/).

156. Philo A. Goodwin, *Biography of Andrew Jackson* (New York: R. Hart Towner, 1833), p. 4.

157. John Quincy Adams, *Memoirs of John Quincy Adams*, Charles Francis Adams, editor (Philadelphia: J. B. Lippincott & Co., 1874), p. 325.

158. *Dictionary of American Biography*, s.v. "Adams, John Quincy."

159. *Dictionary of American Biography*, s.v. "Livingston, William."

160. *Dictionary of American Biography*, s.v. "Iredell, James."

161. Noah Webster, *The Elementary Spelling Book, Being an Improvement on the American Spelling Book* (New York: American Book Company, 1908) pp. 114, 117, 124, 126, 127.

162. Rush, *Essays*, p. 84, "Thoughts upon Female Education, Accommodated to the Present State of Society, Manners, and Government, in the United States of America. Addressed to the Visitors of the Young Ladies' Academy in Philadelphia, 28th July, 1787."

163. H. R. Warfel, *Noah Webster, Schoolmaster to America* (New York: MacMillan Co. 1936), pp. 181-82.